FEASTING ON FLAMES

The best barbecue recipes from

around the world

FEASTING ON FLAMES

The best barbecue recipes from
around the world

Annette Yates

**Eagle
Editions**

A QUANTUM BOOK

Published by Eagle Editions Ltd
11 Heathfield
Royston
Hertfordshire SG8 5BW

Copyright © MCMXCVIII
Quintet Publishing Ltd

This edition printed 2005

ISBN 1-84573-003-8

QUMTGB

Printed in Singapore
by Star Standard Industries (Pte) Ltd

CONTENTS

INTRODUCTION

Just the thought of long summer afternoons and evenings makes barbecuing

seem like an irresistible idea. A quick telephone call to invite friends and family, and then get the barbecue going.

To me, there is nothing more appetizing than the smell of food sizzling on the barbecue. Whether it is at a

spontaneous get-together or a meticulously planned party, barbecued food always conjures up the words

'fresh', 'healthy', 'convivial' and, above all, 'fun'.

BARBECUING CAN BE VERY QUICK, GRILLING SMALL PIECES OF FOOD OVER VERY HOT COALS UNTIL CRISP ON THE OUTSIDE AND SUCCULENT INSIDE, OR IT CAN BE A MORE LENGTHY AFFAIR, SMOKING A LARGE JOINT OF MEAT SLOWLY UNTIL IT SIMPLY FALLS AWAY FROM THE BONE.

IT'S A HEALTHY METHOD OF COOKING TOO, USING VERY LITTLE FAT. ANY FAT THAT EXISTS ON THE FOOD MOSTLY FALLS, WITH THE JUICES, ON TO THE HOT COALS TO PRODUCE THE SMOKE WHICH IMPARTS THAT WONDERFUL BARBECUED FLAVOUR TO THE FOOD.

I SIMPLY LOVE BEING AND COOKING OUTDOORS. GROWING UP IN THE MOUNTAINS OF SOUTH WALES, MY PASSION WAS TO BUILD A SMALL FIRE AND COOK TINY WHOLE POTATOES FOR A SMALL GROUP OF EAGER FRIENDS. SINCE THEN, I HAVE BEEN A DEDICATED OUTDOOR COOK, ENJOYING CAMPING HOLIDAYS MOST SUMMERS. I CAN HONESTLY SAY THAT, GIVEN THE OPPORTUNITY (AND GOOD WEATHER OF COURSE), I WOULD BARBECUE EVERY SINGLE DAY.

THERE'S NO DOUBT ABOUT IT, COOKING OUT-DOORS IS GREAT FUN AS WELL AS BEING A WONDERFUL SOCIAL ACTIVITY.

I HOPE THAT YOU ENJOY THE RECIPES IN THIS BOOK AS MUCH AS I HAVE ENJOYED CREATING THEM. NOW GO ON, GET THE BARBECUE OUT, LIGHT UP AND GET COOKING!

ANNETTE YATES

Chapter 1

RIGHT: KETTLE BARBECUE

The Barbecue

Barbecuing is simply cooking, or smoking food over an open fire. Today's barbecues are generally made up of a box that contains the fire, with a metal grid sitting over it on which the food is cooked. The fats and juices drip from the food on to the heat source, producing the smoke which gives that wonderful, distinctive flavour to the food. Choose from tiny disposable barbecues in foil containers to sophisticated trolleys that include every type of cooking surface and gadget that you could wish for.

ABOVE: PORTABLE BARBECUE

The Right Equipment

*Your basic choices
are charcoal or gas. There are those who would
not be persuaded to use anything other than charcoal, because
for them the building, lighting and nurturing of the fire are all part of the occasion
and the tradition. Others prefer the immediacy of a gas barbecue, which
is usually ready to use about ten minutes after lighting. No matter
which you choose, the food will have that recognizable
'cooked outdoors' flavour.*

Barbecue Designs

DISPOSABLE BARBECUES These are small and inexpensive, designed to be disposed of after use. They are great for small spaces or for a spontaneous barbecue for two, whether in the garden, on the balcony, on the beach or at a campsite. A thin metal grid sits over a foil tray containing charcoal which has been impregnated with lighter fuel. They are easy to light, ready to use in about 15 minutes and last for about an hour. The best foods to cook on them are small, thin pieces such as chops, burgers, sausages, vegetables and kebabs. These are also a good buy for people trying barbecuing for the first time.

PORTABLE BARBECUES
There are four basic designs available.
The Hibachi barbecue (Japanese for fire bowl) has a sturdy, shallow metal tray on short legs or feet, with one or more cooking grids on top. The height of the grids can be adjusted, by slotting them into different notches and they often have convenient wooden handles.

FOLD-AWAY BARBECUES are lightweight and easy to assemble.

BUCKET BARBECUES are just what they say: a metal bucket with a grid placed on the top.

CONVERTIBLE BARBECUES have hot coals sitting below the cooking grid which can be moved into a vertical position to create a back burner for rotisserie cooking.

All these portable versions are great for picnics, the beach, camping or anywhere.

ABOVE: DISPOSABLE BARBECUE
CENTRE: FOLD-AWAY BARBECUE

ABOVE: BUCKET BARBECUE

FREE-STANDING BARBECUES These come in various designs and are made up of a fire bowl on legs with a cooking grid above, which is usually adjustable. The cooking area is larger than that of the portable types. Some have lids, some do not. Kettle, barrel and pedestal or pillar barbecues are the most efficient. They are easy to light, quick to reach cooking temperature and the ventilation can be adjusted to control the rate at which the coals burn. All of them are ideal for the garden.

WAGON OR TROLLEY BARBECUES These are generally large and come in designs which vary from the simple to the glamorous, with or without lids, with some or many utensils and shelves. What they all have in common are wheels which allow you to push them, wheelbarrow style, to where you want to cook. Wagon and trolley barbecues are perfect for garden parties.

CENTRE: FREE-STANDING BARBECUE
ABOVE: TROLLEY BARBECUE

LEFT: KETTLE BARBECUE

PERMANENT BARBECUES A brick-built barbecue makes barbecuing part of your everyday life. It's ideal where the summer weather is guaranteed to be warm and dry. It also provides an attractive patio area or garden feature. The cooking space can be as large and as adjustable as you like, and you can build in shelves, ovens, and storage areas. Simple do-it-yourself kits are available. Cement the bricks to make a permanent barbecue; stack them for a barbecue which can be dismantled at any time.

Buying a Barbecue

COOKING SPACE For regular barbecuers, it's important to have a grill area which is larger than you think you need. Even if you cook only small quantities of food, it allows you to move the food around, to hotter or cooler areas or away from flare-ups. You can move the coals around too, to create hotter or cooler cooking areas.

ADJUSTABLE GRID HEIGHTS These are also useful, so you can adjust the cooking temperature by moving the food closer to or further away from the heat. For the same reason, if you choose the gas variety, it's helpful to be able to adjust the gas flow. The bars on the cooking grids should be sturdy and not so far apart that the food may fall through.

ABOVE: GRILL AREA ON A KETTLE BARBECUE

SAFETY Make sure the barbecue is stable; a wobbly model is a dangerous one. Handles should always be made of wood or a heat-resistant plastic.

LIDS Models with lids are the most versatile, allowing you to grill conventionally or cook the food covered. If you choose a model with a lid, make sure it is deep enough to contain the largest bird or piece of meat that you will want to cook.

CLEANING AND STORAGE Is the barbecue you are thinking of buying easy to clean? You will avoid hours of frustration if it is. You may also need to store the barbecue somewhere during the winter. Take this into account when choosing.

Fuel

CHARCOAL This is wood which has been partly burnt, without igniting it, to produce black, lightweight carbon. There are two main types: lumpwood and briquettes. Other alternatives are available, made from sawdust, sand and various other materials, but I have to admit to preferring charcoal.

LUMPWOOD is very convenient. It lights easily to give a regular, long-lasting fire that burns cleanly, giving slightly more heat than briquettes. I like this type best because it has no additives.

BRIQUETTES are widely available. They are made from compressed particles of charcoal, often with additives which help them to light easily. They give a regular, steady heat and they tend to burn for longer than lumpwood.

BELOW: LUMPWOOD CHARCOAL, SPREAD EVENLY

SELF-IGNITING CHARCOAL is convenient. It is usually sold in a sealed paper bag which is lit from the outside. This makes it useful for starting off the barbecue before adding extra coals.

GAS This is usually liquid petroleum (LP) in the form of butane or propane. Butane is most frequently used, particularly in warm weather. In cooler conditions it is advisable to use propane, which operates well in low temperatures. Natural gas is also available in cylinders, though not in Europe.

If your home has a mains gas supply, it is possible to have an outside fitting for a barbecue, though this does mean that the barbecue will have to be used close to the house.

In a gas barbecue, the flame heats up lumps of lava rock or metal plates or bars. These, in turn, heat the food on the cooking grid above.

Essential extras

YOU WILL NEED:
A thick apron and oven gloves.

Heavy-duty long-handled tongs, slice and mopping brushes (make sure they don't give or bend). They should be long enough to allow you to work over a hot fire without burning your hands or forearms.

Metal and bamboo skewers. The best metal skewers are the flat type, which prevent the food from slipping as you turn it on the barbecue. Bamboo skewers should be soaked in cold water for at least 30 minutes before using to prevent them burning too quickly on the barbecue.

Thick, heavy-duty foil for wrapping foods to be cooked on the barbecue.

Hinged wire grids. Various shapes are available for holding fish, meat or vegetables.

A wire brush for cleaning the grill surface.

A Flaming Success

To achieve consistently good results with your barbecuing, there are a few simple tips that are worth following.

Before You Start

Have several foods to offer your guests that don't need cooking on the barbecue, such as nibbles, dips, sauces, salads and breads. A separate table, away from the barbecue (and preferably in the shade) can hold plates and glasses, cutlery and napkins and all the different foods that will accompany the barbecued pieces.

Prepare as much as you can ahead of time. Make sure everything you need for cooking (ingredients, tools, bastes and oils) is handy on a large sturdy table nearby.

Being organized and efficient results in a confident and calm cook. Why not use your microwave to partly cook some foods before barbecuing? This not only saves time but it also helps to ensure that foods (particularly chicken or pork) are cooked thoroughly.

Flavour Boosting

Supermarket shelves are full of seasonings, marinades, bastes and sauces for the barbecue. Alternatively, make them yourself; there are several quick and easy recipes on pages 18–25.

Another way to flavour food is to throw fresh herbs on to the fire (rosemary and thyme are good). A good variety of aromatic wood chips or chunks is also available commercially (such as hickory, mesquite, maple, apple, cherry, oak and pecan). Using herbs and woods also gives atmosphere to the occasion.

Lighting Up

CHARCOAL Remove the lid from the barbecue, if there is one, and open up the vents. Aim to build a fire that is about as large as the surface area of the food you are cooking. Spread the charcoal, about two layers thick, over the barbecue base, then pile it into a neat heap. Add barbecue lighter fluid, gel or firelighters (they may smell at first but this burns off after about ten minutes). Alternatively, electric starters are very reliable, with no fumes, but you will need an extension lead. Light the coals and leave for about 10 minutes until they glow red. Spread the coals into a even layer over the base and leave them to heat up. This will take about 25 to 35 minutes.

GAS Remove the lid, if there is one, and ignite the burners. Gently close the lid and, following the manufacturer's instructions, leave the barbecue to heat up to cooking temperature.

Now try the hand test. Hold your hand about 13 centimetres/5 inches above the cooking surface. If you can hold it there for 1 to 2 seconds, you have a hot fire; 3 to 5 seconds means a medium fire; 6 to 8 seconds (with no glowing coals) is cool. When you want a cool fire (perhaps for cooking fruit and desserts), it's best to let the charcoal burn for longer and die down a little.

Start cooking only when all the flames have disappeared and the coals are glowing red under a uniform coating of grey ash. A charcoal barbecue takes about 35 to 45 minutes to reach cooking stage; a gas barbecue takes 10 to 15 minutes.

Vigilance

*Keep a constant eye on your fire to make sure that it is
staying at the heat required.*

CHARCOAL Regulate the temperature by moving the food towards, or away from, the fire. Alternatively, move the coals around. To increase the heat, push the coals closer together. To reduce the heat, spread them out a little and partly close the vents.

If you require the barbecue to stay hot for more than an hour, you will need to add more charcoal. Either add pieces around the edges or, once the first batch is lit, light a second batch in an old metal roasting tin and transfer the hot coals to the barbecue with metal tongs. Do not pile cold charcoal on top of the fire, it will only deaden it.

GAS Regulate the temperature by adjusting the gas flow or by moving the food towards or away from the heat.

Sizzling Skills

GRILLING This, probably the simplest method of cooking, is carried out by placing food within a few inches of the direct heat of a fire so it cooks by conduction, searing the food on the outside to seal the juices inside, the crusty brown surface giving the recognizable 'grilled' flavour. Once seared, the food can be moved to the cooler edges of the barbecue to finish cooking.

BARBECUING To most of us this simply means cooking on a grill in the open air. However, to real enthusiasts, true barbecuing is slow smoking over a low fire, with the lid on and the coals spread around the edges only (or the gas turned off in the area directly under the food), to give a really tender result with a smoky flavour. The top of the food is cooked by heat reflected from the inside of the metal lid. This way, it is possible to use tougher cuts of meat which normally have loads of flavour.

SKILLET OR PAN COOKING Use skillets, pans and woks on the barbecue, just as you would when using a conventional hob.

ROTISSERIE COOKING Many portable and larger barbecues incorporate a spit on which you can roast fish, poultry and joints of meat. Follow the manufacturer's instructions when using these.

Cooking Tips

Before you begin any cooking on the barbecue, it is a good idea to brush the cooking grid lightly with oil; this will help to prevent the food from sticking to the grids, which can be very difficult to clean off later.

Leave room between items of food, sufficient to turn and move them to hotter or cooler areas. When using skewers, leave a small amount of space between the food pieces, so they will cook evenly.

Use the cooking times recommended in the recipes in this book as a guide only. They will depend on the heat of the fire, and the thickness and starting temperature of the food, as well as how you like your food cooked.

Check the food frequently while it is cooking, particularly when grilling small, tender pieces. However, if you are slow 'smoking' a large piece of food with the lid on, resist the temptation to peek too frequently. Each time the lid is opened some heat will be lost. To compensate, add a little extra to the total cooking time.

Flare-ups

Flare-ups are caused by fat, juices and marinades dripping on to the fire. Sudden flames leap up at the food to blacken it, giving it a nasty taste. Use a spray bottle of cold water to douse any flames that appear and leave it beside the barbecue during cooking.

Cleaning Up

Any food left stuck to the grids after a barbecue could cause a health hazard and will definitely affect the taste of your next barbecued meal.

Clearing up is best done while the grill is still hot. Brush the cooking grid with a wire brush, allowing the food residues to fall into the dying fire. Should the food refuse to burn off the cooking grid, use hot soapy water and a scouring pad. Once the barbecue has cooled completely, brush out and dispose of the ashes.

Gas barbecues will need their cooking grids and heat plates or bars scraping of old food. Lava rocks can be used over and over again, but they will last longer if they are washed in hot soapy water occasionally, to remove any grease and grime.

Be Safe

Follow the manufacturer's instructions for lighting, using and cleaning the barbecue.

Before cooking make sure you keep all food covered, cool and out of the sun.

Thaw frozen food completely before cooking.

Position the barbecue on a solid, level surface, out of high wind and away from tree branches, bushes, wooden fences and sheds.

Disposable and portable models should be placed on a heatproof surface (bricks are good) or on the ground.

Never light a charcoal barbecue with petrol, methylated spirits, white spirit or paraffin. It's dangerous and will taint and spoil the food.

Open the lid of a gas barbecue before lighting it.

Never apply lighting fluid, gel or firelighters to a charcoal barbecue which has already been lit.

In the unlikely event that the barbecue catches fire, have handy a fire extinguisher or a bucket of sand or garden soil to throw over it.

Do not attempt to move a barbecue which has already been lit.

Never leave a barbecue unattended and don't allow children or animals near it.

Leave the barbecue to cool completely before moving it or packing it away.

Recipe Notes

All spoon measurements are level unless otherwise stated.

Follow one set of measurements only. Metric and imperial quantities are not interchangeable.

Ingredients are conveniently listed in the order in which they are used.

Cooking times are approximate and should be used as a guide only. They will vary according to the starting temperature of the food and its thickness and the heat of the barbecue.

Chapter
2

Marinades
Glazes

Seasonings, & Sauces

Teriyaki Red Wine Marinade

Teriyaki is a Japanese soy sauce which is very smooth and deep flavoured, making it ideal for marinating. In Japanese TERI means 'sunshine' and YAKI means 'roast' or 'grilled', so what could be more suitable for barbecuing? This marinade is particularly good with beef, lamb and duck.

Makes enough for 900 g/2 lb

- 60 ml/4 Tbsp Teriyaki sauce
- 60 ml/4 Tbsp red wine
- 15 ml/1 Tbsp sesame oil
- 15 ml/1 Tbsp finely chopped fresh root ginger
- 2 plump garlic cloves, finely chopped

Mix all the ingredients together and use as required.

Sesame Lime Marinade

The sesame oil in this marinade creates a wonderfully nutty flavour that is balanced by the citric tartness of the lime juice. Use this mixture on chicken, fish and seafood.

Makes enough for 900 g/2 lb

- 30 ml/2 Tbsp sesame oil
- 30 ml/2 Tbsp rice vinegar
- 30 ml/2 Tbsp lime juice
- 30 ml/2 Tbsp light soy sauce
- 10 ml/2 tsp sugar

Mix all the ingredients together and use as required.

Worcestershire and Orange Marinade

This sweet marinade contains Worcestershire sauce, creating a well-rounded flavouring that can be enjoyed especially with pork and chicken.

Makes enough for 900 g/2 lb

- 60 ml/4 Tbsp orange juice
- 60 ml/4 Tbsp clear honey
- 30 ml/2 Tbsp Worcestershire sauce
- 15 ml/1 Tbsp olive oil
- 15 ml/1 Tbsp finely grated orange rind
- 1 plump garlic clove, finely chopped

Mix all the ingredients together and use as required.

RIGHT: TERIYAKI RED WINE MARINADE, WORCESTERSHIRE AND ORANGE MARINADE AND SESAME LIME MARINADE

Mediterranean Rub

The aromatic herb oregano, native to the Mediterranean, is combined with subtle spices in this flavoursome blend. This mix is good with any meat or firm fish.

Makes enough for 900 g/2 lb

- ❖ 75 ml/5 Tbsp olive oil
- ❖ 30 ml/2 Tbsp dried oregano
- ❖ 30 ml/2 Tbsp ground cumin
- ❖ 15 ml/1 Tbsp ground coriander
- ❖ 15 ml/1 Tbsp paprika
- ❖ 15 ml/1 Tbsp ground ginger
- ❖ 5 ml/1 tsp ground black pepper
- ❖ 2.5 ml/½ tsp salt

Mix all the ingredients together.

Rub or brush over your chosen food before barbecuing, then cook over a low heat to prevent the surface from browning too quickly.

Dry Spice Rub

This spicy seasoning will give the barbecued meat a wonderful warm orange colour. It may be enjoyed on pork and chicken.

Makes enough for 900 g/2 lb

- ❖ 55 g/2 oz brown sugar
- ❖ 60 ml/4 Tbsp paprika
- ❖ 20 ml/4 tsp ground cumin
- ❖ 10 ml/2 tsp salt
- ❖ 10 ml/2 tsp ground black pepper
- ❖ 7.5 ml/½ tsp cayenne pepper

Mix all the ingredients together and rub over your chosen food before barbecuing.

Cook over a medium heat to prevent the surface from browning too quickly.

Barbecue Mop

The proportion of vinegar may seem high in this recipe, but don't be put off. Try it on fish, meat or vegetables.

Makes enough for 900 g/2 lb

- ❖ 90 ml/6 Tbsp cider vinegar
- ❖ 45 ml/3 Tbsp water
- ❖ 25 ml/1½ Tbsp Worcestershire sauce
- ❖ 25 ml/1½ Tbsp oil
- ❖ 10 ml/2 tsp salt
- ❖ 10 ml/2 tsp ground black pepper
- ❖ 2.5 ml/1½ tsp cayenne pepper

Mix all the ingredients together. Brush the mixture over the food you have chosen before cooking and then frequently during cooking.

RIGHT: BARBECUE MOP, DRY SPICE RUB AND MEDITERRANEAN RUB

Honey-mustard Glaze

Use a robust wholegrain mustard in this glaze. It provides a wonderful flavour and an interesting texture. It is very good with chicken, turkey, lamb, fish or vegetables.

Makes enough for 900 g/2 lb

- ❖ 60 ml/4 Tbsp clear honey
- ❖ 60 ml/4 Tbsp wholegrain mustard
- ❖ 30 ml/2 Tbsp lemon juice
- ❖ 15 ml/1 Tbsp olive oil
- ❖ 15 ml/1 Tbsp chopped fresh tarragon

Mix all the ingredients together.

Brush the mixture over the food you are cooking during the final 10 to 15 minutes of barbecuing. Cook the food over a medium heat to prevent the glaze from browning too quickly.

The Ultimate Barbecue Sauce

Use this sauce as a glaze too if you wish. Brush it over the barbecuing food halfway through cooking but take care that it does not burn.

Serves 8

- ❖ 15 ml/1 Tbsp olive oil
- ❖ 1 large onion, finely chopped
- ❖ 3 plump garlic cloves, finely chopped
- ❖ 300 ml/½ pt stout
- ❖ 90 ml/6 Tbsp tomato ketchup
- ❖ 60 ml/4 Tbsp tomato purée
- ❖ 60 ml/4 Tbsp Worcestershire sauce
- ❖ 30 ml/2 Tbsp malt vinegar
- ❖ 25 g/1 oz soft brown sugar
- ❖ 30 ml/2 Tbsp Dijon mustard
- ❖ 2.5 ml/½ tsp ground black pepper

Heat the oil in a large pan and add the onion and garlic. Cook over a medium heat for about 5 minutes, stirring frequently, until the onion is soft but not brown.

Add the remaining ingredients and stir well.

Bring to the boil, then cover and simmer gently for 15 to 20 minutes, stirring occasionally.

If the sauce needs thickening, remove the lid and simmer gently for a further 10 minutes or until the sauce reaches the desired consistency.

Apricot and Lime Glaze

The lime juice in this glaze creates a much stronger citrus flavour than lemon juice would, so don't substitute a lemon for the lime. This is especially good on chicken and pork.

Makes enough for 900 g/2 lb

❖ 60 ml/4 Tbsp apricot jam
❖ Finely grated rind of
   1 lime

❖ 60 ml/4 Tbsp lime juice
❖ 10 ml/2 tsp Dijon mustard
❖ Ground black pepper

Mix all the ingredients together.

Brush the glaze over the food during the final 15 minutes of barbecuing. Cook over a medium heat to prevent the glaze from browning too quickly.

Hot Soy Sauce

This glaze is precooked and then brushed over the food during the last few minutes of cooking. It goes well with fish, seafood, chicken or pork.

Makes enough for 900 g/2 lb

❖ 30 ml/2 Tbsp olive oil
❖ 2 fresh red chillies,
   halved, seeds removed
   and finely chopped
❖ 10 ml/2 tsp grated fresh
   root ginger
❖ 2 plump garlic cloves,
   crushed

❖ 150 ml/¼ pt dry white
   wine
❖ 60 ml/4 Tbsp soy sauce
❖ 55 g/2 oz dark soft
   brown sugar
❖ 12.5 ml/2 rounded tsp
   cornflour
❖ 15 ml/1 Tbsp lemon juice

Heat the oil in a pan and add the chillies, ginger and garlic. Cook, stirring frequently, for 1 to 2 minutes without browning.

Whisk together the wine, soy sauce, sugar and cornflour and add to the pan.

ABOVE: HOT SOY SAUCE AND APRICOT AND LIME GLAZE

Bring to the boil, stirring, until thickened. Tip the sauce into a bowl and leave to cool.

Stir the lemon juice into the cooled sauce.

Brush the glaze over the food you are cooking during the final 15 minutes of barbecuing. Cook over a medium heat to prevent the glaze from browning too quickly.

Oriental Sweet and Sour Sauce

There are many different recipes for sweet and sour sauce. This one is particularly delicious with burgers, chops and ribs. It is so easy to prepare and can be made quickly, especially if you use canned tomatoes.

Tip

To skin fresh tomatoes, plunge them into a bowl of just-boiled water for two minutes and then into cold water. The skins will have split. Gently ease them off using your fingers; they should slip off quite easily.

Serves 6–8

- 15 ml/1 Tbsp olive oil
- 1 onion, thinly sliced
- 1 plump garlic clove, finely chopped
- 1 green pepper, seeds removed and sliced
- 400 g/14 oz can chopped tomatoes, or 450 g/1 lb fresh tomatoes, skinned and chopped
- 85 g/3 oz soft brown sugar
- 5 ml/1 tsp mixed dried herbs
- 90 ml/6 Tbsp water
- 225 g/8 oz can pineapple chunks in juice
- 60 ml/4 Tbsp red wine vinegar
- 60 ml/4 Tbsp light soy sauce
- 30 ml/2 Tbsp cornflour
- Salt and ground black pepper

Heat the oil in a pan and add the onion, garlic and pepper. Cook gently for about 5 minutes, stirring occasionally, until the vegetables are soft but not brown.

Stir in the tomatoes, sugar, herbs and water.

Drain the pineapple, adding the juice to the pan.

Whisk together the vinegar, soy sauce and cornflour, and add to the pan.

Bring to the boil, stirring, until the sauce thickens and becomes glossy. Simmer gently for 5 minutes.

Season to taste and add the pineapple chunks. Heat through and serve.

Fresh Tomato Sauce

*This is a sauce for all foods. Serve with fish,
vegetables, meat or poultry. Experiment with different dried herbs
according to the food you are serving.*

Serves 6

- 30 ml/2 Tbsp olive oil
- 1 onion, finely chopped
- 1 small carrot, finely chopped
- 1 plump garlic clove, finely chopped
- 550 g/1¼ lb fresh ripe tomatoes, skinned and chopped
- 350 ml/12 fl oz chicken or vegetable stock
- 15 ml/1 Tbsp caster sugar
- 30 ml/2 Tbsp tomato purée
- 15 ml/1 Tbsp dried herbs, such as thyme, oregano, or a mixture
- Salt and ground black pepper

Heat the oil in a pan and add the onion, carrot and garlic. Cook gently for 5 to 10 minutes, stirring frequently, until very soft but not brown.

Stir in the tomatoes, stock, sugar, tomato purée and herbs. Heat until bubbling, then cover and simmer gently for 20 to 30 minutes.

Season to taste with salt and pepper then tip the sauce into a blender or food processor and whiz until smooth. If you like a really smooth sauce, you can pass it through a nylon sieve.

Adjust the seasoning to taste and reheat before serving.

Coconut Curry Sauce

*Canned coconut milk is now widely available and forms the basis of this tasty sauce.
The fresh coriander imparts a wonderful flavour. It is good served with chicken,
fish, seafood and vegetable kebabs.*

Serves 6

- 15 ml/1 Tbsp curry powder
- 2.5 ml/½ tsp cayenne pepper
- 6 spring onions, sliced
- 400 ml/14 fl oz can coconut milk
- Salt and ground black pepper
- 60 ml/4 Tbsp chopped fresh coriander

Put the curry powder and cayenne pepper into a pan and place over a low heat for a few minutes, shaking the pan frequently, until the mixture begins to toast.

Stir in the onions and coconut milk. Bring to the boil, then simmer gently for about 10 minutes, stirring occasionally.

Season to taste with salt and pepper. Stir in the coriander and serve.

Chapter

3

Fish

& Seafood

Spicy Barbecued Tuna

Tuna is an ideal fish for barbecuing. Its 'meaty' texture means that it holds together well during cooking. As it is a well-flavoured fish, it is complemented by this strong seasoning.

Serves 6

- ❖ 45 ml/3 Tbsp olive oil
- ❖ 45 ml/3 Tbsp tomato purée
- ❖ 45 ml/3 Tbsp red wine vinegar
- ❖ 45 ml/3 Tbsp Worcestershire sauce
- ❖ 45 ml/3 Tbsp Dijon mustard
- ❖ 15 ml/1 Tbsp soft brown sugar
- ❖ Salt and ground black pepper
- ❖ 6 tuna steaks, about 2.5 cm/1 in thick

Tip
Tuna becomes rather dry if overcooked. Stop cooking when it is still slightly translucent at the centre.

Put the first six ingredients into a shallow non-metallic dish, large enough to hold the fish in a single layer. Add seasoning and mix well. Then add the tuna and spoon the sauce over to coat evenly.

Cover and leave to marinate for about 1 hour, turning the tuna over once.

Transfer the sauce-coated tuna steaks to the barbecue and cook over a medium-high heat for 4 to 5 minutes on each side, or until very nearly cooked through (see Tip, left).

Grilled Tuna with Orange, Thyme and Garlic

The flavours of orange and tuna complement each other wonderfully well. In this recipe thin slices of garlic are pushed into the tuna steaks, creating an intensely garlicky dish.

Serves 6

- ❖ Juice of 1 large orange
- ❖ 3 plump garlic cloves, very thinly sliced
- ❖ 30 ml/2 Tbsp fresh thyme leaves
- ❖ 15 ml/1 Tbsp finely grated orange rind
- ❖ Salt and ground black pepper
- ❖ 6 tuna steaks, about 2.5 cm/1 in thick

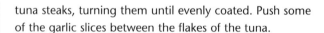

Put the orange juice, garlic, thyme, orange rind and seasoning into a shallow non-metallic dish, large enough to hold the tuna in a single layer. Mix well, then add the tuna steaks, turning them until evenly coated. Push some of the garlic slices between the flakes of the tuna.

Cover and leave to marinate in the fridge for 30 minutes to 1 hour, turning the tuna once or twice during this time.

Lift the fish out of its marinade and cook over a medium-high heat for about 4 to 5 minutes on each side or until very nearly cooked through (see Tip, above).

RIGHT: GRILLED TUNA WITH ORANGE, THYME AND GARLIC

Grilled Swordfish with Pistachio and Olive Butter

*The flavoured butter melts over the hot fish to reveal the shiny black
olives and the pretty green pistachios in this succulent dish.*

Serves 6

- ❖ 6 swordfish steaks, about
  2 cm/¾ in thick
- ❖ Olive oil, for brushing
- ❖ Salt and ground black
  pepper
- ❖ 30 ml/2 Tbsp dried
  oregano

For the butter
- ❖ 55 g/2 oz soft butter
- ❖ 55 g/2 oz pistachios,
  shelled and finely
  chopped
- ❖ 6 stoned black olives,
  sliced into very thin rings
- ❖ 5 ml/1 tsp finely grated
  lemon rind
- ❖ 15 ml/1 Tbsp lemon juice

Brush the fish with olive oil, season lightly with salt and pepper, and sprinkle over the oregano.

Blend the butter with the remaining ingredients and season with ground black pepper.

Cook the swordfish over a medium-high heat for 4 to 5 minutes on each side until just cooked through.

To serve, top each steak with a spoonful of the butter.

Tip
If your barbecue is large enough, you may prefer to heat the butter gently on the side coals, then spoon the melted mixture over the hot fish.

Spiced Swordfish with Avocado and Lime Salsa

*The spices in this dish give a 'dry' flavour to the swordfish which is
complemented by the creamy, moist texture of the salsa.*

Serves 6

- 60 ml/4 Tbsp olive oil
- 15 ml/1 Tbsp paprika
- 15 ml/1 Tbsp ground cumin
- 10 ml/2 tsp grated nutmeg
- 5 ml/1 tsp celery salt
- Salt and ground black pepper
- 6 swordfish steaks, about 2.5 cm/1 in thick

For the salsa
- 1 large ripe avocado
- 20 ml/4 tsp lime juice
- Small red onion, finely chopped
- Finely grated rind of 1 small lime
- 1 fresh red chilli, finely chopped
- 30 ml/2 Tbsp finely chopped fresh parsley

Mix together the oil, paprika, cumin, nutmeg and celery salt. Season with ground black pepper. Rub the mixture over the swordfish steaks, cover and leave in the fridge for about 1 hour.

To make the salsa, halve the avocado, remove the stone and peel. Cut the flesh into small dice and put into a bowl. Sprinkle with the lime juice and stir gently. Add the onion, lime rind, chilli and parsley. Season to taste. Mix gently, cover and leave to stand.

Transfer the swordfish to the barbecue and cook over a medium-high heat for 4 to 5 minutes on each side, until just cooked through.

Serve immediately with the salsa.

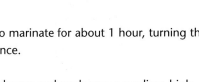

Grilled Sardines with Lemon and Chilli

*Serve these spicy sardines with a salad of watercress and orange
segments, drizzled with an oil and vinegar dressing.*

Serves 6

- 12 or 18 sardines, depending on their size, cleaned
- Salt and ground black pepper
- 30 ml/2 Tbsp olive oil
- Finely grated rind and juice of 1 lemon
- 2 fresh red chillies
- Lemon wedges, to serve

Sprinkle the sardines with salt and lay them, in a single layer, in a shallow non-metallic dish. Drizzle the oil over them, followed by the lemon juice. Sprinkle with pepper and the lemon rind.

Cut the chillies into thin slivers, discarding the seeds (or leave them in if you like a really fiery flavour). Scatter over the fish, then move them around to make sure that each one is coated with at least some of the other ingredients. Brush some of the mixture inside the fish too.

Cover and leave to marinate for about 1 hour, turning the sardines at least once.

Transfer to the barbecue and cook over a medium-high heat for 3 to 4 minutes on each side, until the skin becomes crisp and crunchy.

Serve immediately with lemon wedges for squeezing over.

Thai-style Butterfly Jumbo Prawns

Although this recipe serves four as a main course, it is also great as a starter.
Thread three or four prawns on to small presoaked wooden skewers, cook as
directed and serve on a bed of shredded lettuce.

Serves 4

- ❖ 24 large raw prawns
- ❖ 300 ml/½ pt coconut milk
- ❖ 4 large spring onions
- ❖ 5 cm/2 in piece fresh root ginger, peeled and chopped
- ❖ 2 plump garlic cloves
- ❖ 2 fresh red chillies
- ❖ Finely grated rind of 1 lime
- ❖ 30 ml/2 Tbsp lime juice
- ❖ Several large sprigs of coriander
- ❖ Salt and ground black pepper

Peel the prawns, leaving the tails intact. Make a cut down the back of each, remove the thin black vein, then open the prawns out into the shape of a butterfly.
Put the remaining ingredients into a blender or food processor and whiz until smooth.

Pour the mixture over the prawns, stirring to coat well. Cover and leave to marinate for 30 minutes to 1 hour.

Thread the prawns on to skewers then cook over a medium-high heat for about 5 minutes, turning once or twice, until just firm and opaque. Serve immediately.

34

Tuna and Scallop Brochettes

*Serve these delicious brochettes on their skewers or slip them off and
present them on a bed of rice with a mixed salad on the side.*

Serves 6

- 18 scallops
- 90 ml/6 Tbsp flavoured oil, such as chilli or tarragon
- 30 ml/2 Tbsp red wine vinegar
- 30 ml/2 Tbsp tomato purée
- Salt and ground black pepper
- 675 g/1½ lb tuna steaks, cut into 4 cm/ 1½ in chunks

Tip the scallops into a saucepan of boiling water for 1 minute, drain and leave to cool (this helps prevent them sticking to the barbecue grid).

In a large bowl, whisk together the oil, vinegar, tomato purée and seasoning. Add the scallops and tuna, stirring until well coated.

Thread alternately on to skewers, then cook over a medium-high heat for about 6 minutes, turning occasionally, until just cooked through. Serve immediately.

Creole Blackened Fish

*Creole cuisine, originating in the West Indies, uses
pungent spices and other flavourings. This dish is a fine example of this
regional cookery.*

Serves 6

- 15 ml/1 Tbsp olive oil
- 10 ml/2 tsp Worcestershire sauce
- 10 ml/2 tsp fresh thyme leaves
- 5 ml/1tsp celery salt
- 5 ml/1 tsp paprika
- 5 ml/1 tsp ground black pepper
- 5 ml/1 tsp brown sugar
- 1 plump garlic clove, crushed
- Pinch of cayenne pepper
- 6 fish fillets with their skin, such as bass, bream, gurnard or mullet

Mix all the ingredients together except the fish and brush or rub all over the fish. Cover and leave to stand for 30 minutes to 1 hour.

Transfer the fillets to the barbecue, skin side up, and cook over a medium-high heat for 1 to 2 minutes until they become lightly browned.

Carefully turn the fish over and continue cooking them for 3 to 5 minutes or until the skin is blackened and crisp. Serve immediately.

Paella

A one-dish meal, paella provides a wonderful variety of tastes and textures. Let people help themselves straight from the pan.

Serves 8

- 90 ml/6 Tbsp olive oil, plus extra for brushing
- 45 ml/3 Tbsp lemon juice
- 30 ml/2 Tbsp clear honey
- 8 chicken thighs
- 16 large whole raw prawns
- 350 g/12 oz fresh mussels
- 150 ml/¼ pt dry white wine, plus 45 ml/ 3 Tbsp for the mussels
- 55 g/2 oz butter
- 1 onion, finely chopped
- 2 red peppers, seeds removed and sliced
- 2 plump garlic cloves, finely chopped
- 450 g/1 lb risotto rice, such as Arborio or carnaroli
- About 1 litre/1¾ pt hot vegetable or chicken stock
- 4 fresh tomatoes, skinned and chopped
- 2.5 ml/½ tsp ground saffron
- Salt and ground black pepper
- 45 ml/3 Tbsp chopped fresh parsley
- Lemon wedges, to serve

Whisk together 3 tablespoons of the olive oil with the lemon juice and honey, and set aside. Brush the chicken thighs and the prawns with oil. Pile the mussels into a double layer of thick foil, then add the 3 tablespoons wine and the butter. Wrap loosely (you need to allow space for the mussels to expand as they open), closing the parcel and gathering the seams towards the top.

Heat the remaining oil in a large paella dish or shallow pan and add the onion, peppers and garlic. Cook gently for about 10 minutes, stirring frequently, until the vegetables are soft but not brown.

Add the rice and cook for 1 to 2 minutes, stirring.

Pour over one-quarter of the hot stock and the remaining wine, then stir in the tomatoes, saffron and seasoning. Heat, stirring occasionally, until the mixture comes to the boil. Then simmer gently for about 20 minutes, adding

extra hot stock each time the rice has absorbed most of the liquid, until the rice is plump and tender. Do not allow the rice to dry out completely; it should be quite moist.

Meanwhile, cook the chicken over a medium-high heat for 15 to 20 minutes, turning occasionally, until crisp and cooked through.

Ten minutes after starting to cook the chicken, add the mussel foil parcel, seam side up, and the prawns to the barbecue. Cook over a medium-high heat for about 10 minutes, turning the prawns occasionally (but not the parcel), until you can hear the mussels sizzling and the parcel feels full, and the prawns are pink and cooked.

Add the oil and lemon dressing to the rice. Tear open the foil parcel and tip the mussels and their buttery juices into the rice (discard any mussels that have not opened). Add the chicken, prawns and parsley and stir gently. Serve immediately with lemon wedges for squeezing over.

Tip

Only the size of your barbecue will limit this dish. If you have a large grid area, you will be able to add extra grilled vegetables.

If your barbecue is small, cook the rice in advance, add the oil and lemon dressing and leave it to cool to room temperature. Then cook all the extras on the barbecue and pile them, hot, on top of the cooled rice.

RIGHT: PAELLA

Salmon Fillets with Lime and Coriander

*Like tuna, salmon has a 'meaty' texture that is well
suited to barbecuing. Here salmon cutlets or fillets are combined with the
sharp flavours of lime and fresh coriander to create a tantalizing dish
that is surprisingly easy to achieve.*

Serves 6

- ❖ 4 sun-dried tomatoes in oil, drained and finely chopped
- ❖ 90 ml/6 Tbsp tomato oil or a mixture of olive and tomato oil
- ❖ 45 ml/3 Tbsp chopped fresh coriander

- ❖ 25 ml/1½ Tbsp finely chopped fresh root ginger
- ❖ 25 ml/1½ Tbsp grated lime rind
- ❖ Juice of 1 lime
- ❖ Salt and ground black pepper
- ❖ 6 salmon cutlets or skinless fillets

Tip

Use a hinged wire rack to cook the salmon.

Put the first six ingredients into a non-metallic dish, large enough to hold all of the salmon in a single layer. Add the seasoning and mix in well. Then add the salmon to the bowl and using your fingers, rub the mixture all over the fish.

Cover and leave to marinate for about 1 hour, turning the fish over once or twice.

Transfer the salmon to the barbecue and cook over a medium-high heat for 8 to 10 minutes, turning occasionally, until just cooked through. Serve immediately.

Tropical Fish Skewers

*These kebabs combine succulent prawns, fish and pineapple.
Try adding other fresh fruit, such as fresh mango, to the skewers too.*

Serves 6

- ❖ 18 raw king prawns
- ❖ 675 g/1½ lb firm fish, such as monkfish
- ❖ 45 ml/3 Tbsp olive oil
- ❖ Finely grated rind and juice of 1 lime
- ❖ 15 ml/1 Tbsp finely

- chopped fresh root ginger
- ❖ 30 ml/2 Tbsp clear honey
- ❖ 30 ml/2 Tbsp chopped fresh parsley
- ❖ Salt and ground black pepper
- ❖ 1 small fresh pineapple

Peel the prawns, leaving the tails intact. Cut the fish into 4 centimetre/1½ inch cubes.

Put the oil, lime rind and juice, ginger, honey, salt and pepper and parsley into a large bowl and whisk well. Add the prawns and fish. Cover and leave to marinate in the fridge for about 2 hours, stirring occasionally.

Peel and core the pineapple and cut into chunks (you will probably have too much, but don't waste it, keep some to serve as a dessert).

Thread the prawns, fish and pineapple alternately on to skewers. Cook over a medium-high heat for about 10 minutes, turning occasionally, or until the prawns are just firm and opaque, and the fish is cooked through. Serve immediately.

LEFT: TROPICAL FISH SKEWERS

Salmon and Tomato Parcels

Here salmon fillets are wrapped in foil before cooking. Serve each person with an unopened parcel and just wait for them to appreciate the wonderful aroma that wafts up to greet them!

Serves 6

* Butter, for greasing
* 6 skinless salmon fillets, about 4 cm/1½ in thick
* 6 fresh tomatoes
* 6 spring onions, chopped

* 30 ml/2 Tbsp olive oil
* 15 ml/1 Tbsp lemon juice
* 5 ml/1 tsp caster sugar
* Whole or chopped herbs, such as dill, coriander and parsley

Butter 6 largish sheets of thick foil. Lay each salmon fillet on a sheet of foil. Cut each tomato into about 6 wedges and pile them on top of the salmon. Scatter the onions over the tomatoes.

Whisk together the oil, lemon juice and sugar and drizzle over the top. Finally, add a few sprigs of herbs, or some chopped herbs, to each parcel.

Close the parcels, securing the seams well then cook over a medium-high heat for 8 to 10 minutes, turning the parcels occasionally. Serve immediately.

Lobster Tails with Lemon and Tarragon Sauce

The tangy sauce complements the delicate flavour of the lobster tails exceptionally well.
Whole, cooked and halved lobsters are good served this way too.

Serves 4

❖ **4 uncooked lobster tails**

For the sauce
❖ **55 g/2 oz butter**
❖ **60 ml/4 Tbsp lemon juice**

❖ **15 ml/1 Tbsp finely grated lemon rind**
❖ **60 ml/4 Tbsp snipped fresh chives**
❖ **30 ml/2 Tbsp chopped fresh tarragon**

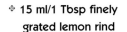

Place the lobster tails in a shallow dish.

To make the sauce, put the butter into a small pan and add the lemon juice and lemon rind. Heat gently until melted, then stir in the herbs.

Brush the butter sauce generously over the lobster tails then transfer them to the barbecue. Cook over a medium-high heat for about 8 to 10 minutes, turning occasionally and brushing with more butter sauce, until the lobster is just opaque.

Reheat any remaining butter sauce and serve separately.

Trout Wrapped in Smoked Bacon

This recipe is based on a traditional Welsh dish. It is ideal for the barbecue.

Serves 4

- 4 whole trout, each weighing about 225 g/ 8 oz, gutted
- Salt and ground black pepper
- 60 ml/4 Tbsp chopped fresh sage
- 1 small lemon, thinly sliced
- 8 rashers (slices) of smoked streaky bacon, rinds removed

Wash and dry the fish thoroughly. Season, inside and out, with salt and pepper.

Sprinkle half the sage inside the fish cavities and insert some lemon slices in each.

With the flat of a knife, stretch the bacon rashers until they are quite thin but still in one piece. Scatter the remaining sage over the trout, then wrap two bacon rashers, spiral-style, around each.

Cook over medium heat for about 5 minutes on each side or until the bacon is crisp and the fish is cooked through. Serve immediately.

Sea Bass with Shallots and Herbs

One fish serves four people here but if you wish to present each person with his or her own fish, use red or grey mullet instead of the sea bass.

Serves 4

- 1 sea bass, weighing about 1.5 kg/3¼ lb, cleaned, scaled and fins removed
- Salt and ground black pepper
- 25 g/1 oz butter, plus 15 g/1 Tbsp for brushing
- 8 shallots, finely chopped
- 120 ml/8 Tbsp chopped fresh herbs, such as dill, coriander and parsley
- Lemon wedges, to serve

Make several diagonal slashes down each side of the fish. Season, inside and out, with salt and pepper.

Heat the 25 grams/1 ounce butter in a small pan until melted. Add the shallots and cook gently for 3 to 5 minutes until soft but not brown. Remove from the heat and stir in the herbs.

Push small spoonfuls of the shallot mixture into the cuts and put any remaining inside the fish.

Melt the 15 grams/1 tablespoon butter and brush over the skin of the fish. Then cook over a medium-high heat for about 10 minutes on each side until just cooked through. Serve immediately with lemon wedges for squeezing over.

Tip
The fins of sea bass are extremely sharp so, if you, rather than the fishmonger, clean the fish, take care not to stab yourself when removing them.

RIGHT: SEA BASS WITH SHALLOTS AND HERBS

Chapter

4

Poultry

Maple-glazed Chicken

*Maple syrup has a unique taste, so make sure you buy the
pure variety and not maple-flavoured syrup. If you cannot find
it, it would be better to use clear honey instead.*

Serves 8

- ❖ 90 ml/6 Tbsp olive oil
- ❖ 90 ml/6 Tbsp maple syrup
- ❖ 25 g/1 oz soft dark
  brown sugar
- ❖ 15 ml/1 Tbsp red wine
  vinegar
- ❖ 15 ml/1 Tbsp dried
  oregano
- ❖ 2 plump garlic cloves,
  crushed
- ❖ 8 chicken drumsticks
- ❖ 8 chicken thighs

In a large bowl, mix together the oil, syrup, sugar,
vinegar, oregano and garlic.

Add the chicken and stir until well coated. Cover and
leave to stand for about 30 minutes.

Transfer the chicken to the barbecue and cook over a
medium-high heat for about 20 minutes, turning the
pieces occasionally, or until crisp, golden brown and
cooked through.

Chicken Tikka

These chicken pieces are good served on a bed of shredded crisp lettuce, with lemon wedges for squeezing over and mango chutney on the side.

Serves 6

❖ 90 ml/6 Tbsp natural yoghurt
❖ 1 small onion, finely chopped
❖ 2 plump garlic cloves, crushed
❖ 30 ml/2 Tbsp garam masala
❖ 30 ml/2 Tbsp lemon juice
❖ 5 ml/1 tsp finely grated lemon rind
❖ 15 ml/1 Tbsp grated fresh root ginger
❖ 5 ml/1 tsp malt vinegar
❖ 5 ml/1 tsp paprika
❖ 5 ml/1 tsp salt
❖ 6 part-boned chicken breasts, with their skins

Put all the ingredients except the chicken pieces into a large, shallow non-metallic dish and mix well. Then using a sharp knife, make several slashes in the skin side of the chicken breasts.

Add the chicken to the yoghurt mixture. Use your hands to turn the pieces, making sure they are well coated and working the mixture into the slashes.

Cover the dish and leave to marinate for up to 2 hours at room temperature, turning the chicken occasionally. (If you wish to leave the chicken longer, put it in the fridge.)

Transfer the chicken to the barbecue and cook over a medium-high heat for about 25 minutes, turning occasionally, until golden brown and cooked through.

Mediterranean-style Poussins

This dish needs to be cooked on a covered barbecue, to ensure that the poussins are cooked through yet remain gloriously moist and succulent.

Serves 4

- ❖ 55 g/2 oz soft butter
- ❖ 25 g/1 oz prosciutto, finely chopped
- ❖ 30 ml/2 Tbsp finely chopped fresh rosemary
- ❖ 2 sun-dried tomatoes in oil, drained and finely chopped
- ❖ 10 ml/2 tsp Dijon mustard
- ❖ Salt and ground black pepper
- ❖ 2 poussins, each weighing about 550–675 g/1¼–1½ lb
- ❖ 1 small lemon

Put the butter, prosciutto, rosemary, tomatoes and mustard into a bowl and mix until well blended.

Season the poussins lightly with salt and pepper.

Carefully lift the skin from the breast of each, running one or two fingers underneath to make a pocket. Spoon half the butter mixture into each pocket and smooth the skin to make a level surface.

Wrap each bird in oiled thick foil, securing the seams well, then cook over a medium heat for about 30 minutes, turning occasionally.

After this time, turn the birds breast side up and (wearing oven gloves) tear open the top of each foil parcel, completely exposing the birds but holding the juices in the foil. Cover the barbecue with its lid and continue cooking for a further 15 minutes or until the poussins are golden brown and cooked through.

Spatchcocked Chicken

Cooking a bird spatchcocked is ideal for barbecuing as it means that it is easier to ensure the meat is cooked through. And it looks attractive too.

Serves 4

- ❖ 1.5 kg/3 lb chicken
- ❖ 45 ml/3 Tbsp olive oil
- ❖ 2 plump garlic cloves, crushed
- ❖ Finely grated rind of 1 lemon
- ❖ 15 ml/1 Tbsp jalapeño chilli sauce
- ❖ 5 ml/1 tsp paprika
- ❖ Salt and ground black pepper

Using poultry shears or strong kitchen scissors, remove the parson's nose from the bird. Turn the chicken breast side down. Cut through the ribs along each side of the backbone and remove it. Open up the chicken and turn it breast side up. Using the heel of your hand, press the bird flat so that the wishbone breaks. Secure the flat shape by inserting two long metal skewers diagonally through the chicken. Lay it in a large, shallow non-metallic dish. Whisk the remaining ingredients together and pour the mixture over the chicken, brushing it into every surface until well coated. Cover and leave to marinate in the fridge for 2 hours or overnight if wished, turning once or twice during this time.

Transfer to the barbecue and cook over a medium-high heat for about 35 minutes, turning occasionally and brushing with any extra marinade, until the skin is really crisp and the chicken is cooked through.

RIGHT: SPATCHCOCKED CHICKEN

Tex-Mex Wings

*This is an economical dish to prepare for a party, as
chicken wings are cheap. So be ready to make double, or even more,
quantities, have plenty of napkins on hand and enjoy!*

Serves 6

* Finely grated rind and juice of 2 oranges
* 15 ml/1 Tbsp malt vinegar
* 45 ml/3 Tbsp black treacle
* 15 ml/1 Tbsp ground coriander
* 15 ml/1 Tbsp Tabasco sauce, or to taste
* 24 chicken wings

Put the orange juice and rind into a large non-metallic bowl. Whisk in the vinegar, treacle, coriander and Tabasco sauce. Add the chicken wings and toss until well coated.

Cover and chill for about 2 hours, stirring occasionally.

Lift the wings out of the marinade and cook over a medium-high heat for 20 to 25 minutes, turning occasionally and basting with the remaining marinade, until crisp and cooked through.

Tip
Make it easier to turn the wings on the barbecue by threading them on to long, flat metal skewers. Alternatively, use a hinged basket.

Texan Drumsticks

*These drumsticks are just delicious. Make sure there are plenty of paper
napkins on hand for people to wipe their fingers.*

Serves 8

* 60 ml/4 Tbsp tomato ketchup
* 30 ml/2 Tbsp light soy sauce
* 30 ml/2 Tbsp black treacle
* 10 ml/2 tsp paprika
* 2 plump garlic cloves, crushed
* Salt and ground black pepper
* 16 chicken drumsticks

In a large, shallow non-metallic dish, mix together the ketchup, soy sauce, treacle, paprika and garlic. Season with salt and pepper then add the chicken and turn the pieces to coat them well.

Cover and leave to marinate for up to 2 hours at room temperature or in the fridge if you are leaving it for longer, turning occasionally.

Transfer the chicken to the barbecue and cook over a medium-high heat for 15 to 20 minutes, turning the drumsticks occasionally, until crisp, slightly charred and cooked through.

LEFT: TEX-MEX WINGS

Bacon-wrapped Chicken with Orange and Walnut Stuffing

The bacon bastes the chicken breasts as they cook, ensuring a mouth-watering, succulent result. Use good quality bacon for the best results.

Serves 8

* 55 g/2 oz butter
* 1 small onion, finely chopped
* Grated rind and juice of 1 orange
* 115 g/4 oz fresh breadcrumbs
* 30 ml/2 Tbsp chopped fresh parsley
* 25 g/1 oz chopped walnuts
* Salt and ground black pepper
* 8 boneless chicken breasts, with their skins
* 8 rashers streaky bacon, rinds removed

To make the stuffing, melt the butter in a small pan and add the onion. Cook gently for about 5 minutes until soft but not brown.

Put the remaining stuffing ingredients into a bowl and add the contents of the pan. Stir well.

Using your fingers, lift one side of skin on each chicken breast, forming a pocket. Fill with the stuffing.

Use the flat side of a knife blade to stretch each bacon rasher to twice its original length. Wrap one piece, spiral style, around each chicken breast and secure with a small metal skewer.

Cook over a medium-high heat for about 25 minutes, turning occasionally, until crisp on the outside and cooked through.

Turkey Kebabs with Mint Marinade

These kebabs are good served with a salad of diced tomatoes, cucumber and spring onions, dressed with vinaigrette and a few chopped mint leaves scattered over the top. This dish is equally good made with strips of chicken breast.

Serves 6

* 90 ml/6 Tbsp olive oil
* 90 ml/6 Tbsp mint jelly
* 3 plump garlic cloves, crushed (optional)
* Salt and ground black pepper
* 900 g/2 lb turkey breast fillets

Put the oil and mint jelly into a small pan and heat gently until the jelly has melted. Stir in the garlic, if using, and season with salt and pepper. Leave to cool.

Cut the turkey into strips about 2.5 centimetres/1 inch wide and put into a large shallow dish. Pour the cooled mint mixture over the turkey and stir until well coated. Cover and leave to marinate for 2 hours at room temperature or chilled for longer, stirring occasionally. Thread the turkey strips, concertina style, on to bamboo skewers (see Tip, below). Cook over a medium-high heat for about 10 minutes, turning frequently and basting with the remaining mint marinade until cooked through.

Tip
Soak the bamboo skewers in cold water for 30 minutes before using, to prevent them burning.

RIGHT: TURKEY KEBABS WITH MINT MARINADE

Cheese-stuffed Turkey Burgers

These burgers are delicious served in split rolls, toasted on the side of the barbecue, with a garnish
of lettuce leaves and tomato slices. Pass round some extra Dijon mustard too.

Serves 4

- 500 g/1 lb 2 oz minced turkey
- 55 g/2 oz fresh breadcrumbs
- 4 spring onions
- 30 ml/2 Tbsp chopped fresh herbs, such as tarragon or dill
- 15 ml/1 Tbsp Dijon mustard
- 1 small egg, lightly beaten
- 2.5 ml/½ tsp salt
- 2.5 ml/½ tsp ground black pepper
- 85 g/3 oz Cheddar cheese, cut into 4 cubes
- Olive oil, for brushing

In a large bowl, combine the first eight ingredients, mixing well. Using your hands, divide the mixture into four and shape into balls.

Push a cube of cheese into the centre of each ball, seal the opening, then carefully shape them into burgers about 10 centimetres/4 inches in diameter. Cover and chill for 2 hours.

Brush the burgers with olive oil and cook over a medium-high heat for about 6 minutes on each side. They are cooked when the meat shrinks to show a few small cracks and the cheese begins to seep out.

Cajun Duck with Soured Cream Dressing

Cajun cookery originated in Louisiana. It is renowned for its use of spices and other flavourings, as illustrated in this delicious recipe.

Serves 4

- 4 meaty duck breasts, weighing about 900 g/2 lb in total
- 45 ml/3 Tbsp olive oil
- 2 plump garlic cloves, finely chopped
- 2 small celery sticks, finely chopped
- 15 ml/1 Tbsp ground coriander
- 15 ml/1 Tbsp dried mixed herbs
- 7.5 ml/1½ tsp ground cumin
- 5 ml/1 tsp chilli powder
- 5 ml/1 tsp caster sugar
- Salt and ground black pepper
- 150 ml/¼ pt soured cream
- 60 ml/4 Tbsp snipped fresh chives or chopped fresh coriander

Remove the skin from the duck breasts. Put one piece of meat between two sheets of clear film. Using a rolling pin, beat and flatten the duck breast until about twice its original size. Repeat with the remaining breasts then lay them in a large shallow dish.

Put the remaining ingredients, except the cream and herbs, into a blender or food processor and whiz until smooth. Pour the mixture over the duck, turning until well coated. Cover and leave to stand for 2 hours at room temperature or chilled for longer, turning occasionally.

Tip the cream into a bowl and stir in the herbs. Cover and chill until required.

Transfer the duck to the barbecue and cook over a high heat for 2 to 3 minutes on each side, until slightly charred and just cooked. Serve immediately with the dressing.

Tip

In this, and the next, recipe the duck skin is removed. When cooking duck with its skin on, cook over a medium-low heat or high above the coals. The fat must have the chance to drip off slowly and evenly, otherwise major flare-ups are likely to occur. Leaving plenty of space between the pieces allows you to move them away from flames if necessary.

Turkey Breasts with Mint and Maple

These turkey steaks are good served with a salad of thinly sliced ripe tomatoes,
scattered with plenty of snipped chives and a few black olives.

Serves 6

❖ **6 turkey breast steaks, about 2.5 cm/1 in thick**
❖ **150 ml/¼ pt Greek yoghurt**
❖ **60 ml/4 Tbsp finely chopped fresh mint**
❖ **45 ml/3 Tbsp maple syrup**
❖ **Salt and ground black pepper**

Put one turkey steak between two sheets of clear film. Using a rolling pin, beat and flatten the turkey steak until about twice its original size. Repeat with the remaining steaks then lay them in a large shallow dish.

Blend together the yoghurt, mint, syrup and seasoning and pour the mixture over the turkey. Move the pieces around so that they are all thoroughly coated. Cover and leave to stand for about 30 minutes.

Transfer the turkey to the barbecue and cook over a medium-high heat for about 3 minutes on each side until golden brown and cooked through.

Duck and Apricot Skewers

The hearty, sweet flavour of duck is perfectly partnered
with the slightly acidic taste of fresh apricots. Make sure the fruit is not
overripe, or it will disintegrate during cooking.

Serves 4

❖ **4 meaty duck breasts, weighing about 900 g/2 lb in total**
❖ **8 firm fresh apricots**
❖ **60 ml/4 Tbsp light soy sauce**
❖ **60 ml/4 Tbsp orange marmalade**
❖ **Ground black pepper**

Skin the duck and cut the flesh into 4 centimetre/1½ inch pieces. Halve the apricots and remove their stones.

In a bowl, mix together the soy sauce and marmalade until well blended. Season with pepper.

Add the duck and apricots to the prepared orange mixture, stirring until well coated. Cover and leave to marinate for 2 hours at room temperature or in the fridge for longer, stirring occasionally.

Thread the duck and apricots alternately on to flat metal skewers then cook over a medium-high heat for 10 to 15 minutes, turning occasionally, depending on how well done you like your duck.

RIGHT: DUCK AND APRICOT SKEWERS

Chapter 5

Meat

Lamb with Mustard and Thyme Crust

*These chops make wonderful finger food. You could make them easier to handle
by scraping the meat off the tip of the bone before cooking.*

Serves 6

❖ 12 lamb loin chops
❖ 60 ml/4 Tbsp olive oil
❖ 60 ml/4 Tbsp wholegrain
   mustard

❖ 60 ml/4 Tbsp fresh thyme
   leaves
❖ 15 ml/1 Tbsp ground
   coriander
❖ Salt and ground black
   pepper

LEFT: LAMB WITH MUSTARD AND THYME CRUST

Put the chops into a shallow, non-metallic dish, large enough to accommodate them in a single layer.

Whisk the remaining ingredients together and pour over the chops, turning until well coated. It is not necessary to leave them to stand, although you can if you wish, making sure they are covered.

Transfer to the barbecue and cook over a medium-high heat for about 15 minutes, turning occasionally, until cooked to your liking.

Butterfly Lamb with Garlic, Lemon and Rosemary

*The shape of the boned lamb resembles butterfly wings,
hence the name of this dish. If you don't fancy boning the lamb yourself,
ask your butcher to do it for you.*

Serves 6–8

❖ 2 kg/4½ lb leg of lamb
❖ 1 lemon
❖ 3 plump garlic cloves,
   sliced

❖ 45 ml/3 Tbsp fresh small
   rosemary sprigs
❖ 45 ml/3 Tbsp olive oil,
   plus extra for brushing
❖ Ground black pepper

On the side where the bone lies just under the surface, make a cut along the bone. Using a very sharp knife, ease the meat away, cutting around the extra bones at the top end of the leg, until you can lift them all out. The meat should open up into the shape of butterfly wings. Trim off any excess fat and, make a few small cuts to make the meat about 6 centimetres/2½ inches thick all over. Make several small, deep incisions over both sides of the lamb.

Using a vegetable peeler or small sharp knife, thinly pare the rind from the lemon and cut into small strips. Halve the lemon and squeeze out its juice.

Into each slit in the lamb, insert a piece of lemon rind, with a slice of garlic and a sprig of rosemary. Lay the meat in a large, shallow, non-metallic dish.

Whisk the oil and lemon, and season with black pepper. Pour over the lamb and brush it over every surface. Cover and leave to marinate for 1 to 2 hours.

Transfer the lamb to the barbecue and cook over a medium-high heat for 40 to 50 minutes, turning occasionally and brushing with any extra marinade, or until the lamb is cooked to your liking.

When the lamb is cooked, lift it on to a serving platter. Keep it warm next to the barbecure and leave to rest for 5 minutes before carving.

Lamb Kefethes

These Greek lamb skewers are delicious served in pitta bread with shredded lettuce and cucumber slices.
Add a spoonful of natural yoghurt with some chopped mint mixed into it.

Serves 6

- 675 g/1½ lb lean minced lamb
- 75 g/2¾ oz fresh breadcrumbs
- 1 large egg
- 1 large onion, grated
- 2 plump garlic cloves, crushed
- Salt and ground black pepper

- About 120 ml/8 Tbsp mixed chopped fresh herbs, such as mint and parsley
- Olive oil, for brushing

Put all the ingredients, except the olive oil, into a large bowl and mix together. Using your hands, divide the mixture into six portions. Take each portion and squeeze it along a flat metal skewer to make a sausage shape, 15–20 centimetres/6–8 inches long.

Cover and chill for 2 hours, or longer if wished.

Brush the meat with a little olive oil, then cook over a medium-high heat for 8 to 10 minutes, turning occasionally, until cooked through.

Lamb Burgers with a Hint of Curry

These burgers are good served with mango chutney or Two-tomato Salsa
(see page 106).

Serves 6

- 15 ml/1 Tbsp olive oil, plus extra for brushing
- 1 onion, finely chopped
- 30 ml/2 Tbsp hot curry paste
- 675 g/1½ lb lean minced lamb
- 5 ml/1 tsp salt

- Ground black pepper
- 75 g/2¾ oz fresh breadcrumbs
- 45 ml/3 Tbsp chopped coriander
- 15 ml/1 Tbsp lemon juice
- 1 large egg, lightly beaten

Heat the oil in a pan and add the onion. Cook for about 5 minutes, stirring occasionally, until soft and light golden brown. Stir in the curry paste, tip the mixture into a large bowl and leave to cool.

Add the remaining ingredients to the cooled onion mixture and combine well.

Using your hands, divide the mixture into six portions and shape into burgers about 4 centimetres/1½ inches thick. Cover and chill for 2 hours, or longer if wished.

Brush lightly with olive oil and cook over a medium-high heat for about 5 minutes on each side or until the lamb is cooked to your liking.

Tip

Using a hinged wire grid makes it easier to turn all the burgers at once. It keeps them in shape too.

RIGHT: LAMB KEFETHES

Texan Steaks with Horseradish Dressing

For "Texan" read "hearty". You will need to be hungry to manage one of these steaks,
which are served accompanied with a feisty sauce.

Serves 4

- ❖ 4 T-bone steaks, about
   2 cm/¾ in thick
- ❖ 60 ml/4 Tbsp red wine
- ❖ 30 ml/2 Tbsp olive oil
- ❖ 30 ml/2 Tbsp soy sauce
- ❖ 45 ml/3 Tbsp chopped
   fresh sage

For the dressing

- ❖ 150 ml/¼ pt soured cream
- ❖ 10 ml/2 tsp creamed
   horseradish
- ❖ Salt and ground black
   pepper
- ❖ 3 spring onions

Put the steaks into a shallow non-metallic dish, large enough to hold the steaks in a single layer (you may need two). Mix together the wine, oil, soy sauce and sage and pour evenly making sure you cover the steaks. Cover and leave to marinate for 1 hour or longer, turning the steaks occasionally.

Meanwhile, make the dressing. Put the cream into a bowl and stir in the horseradish. Season to taste. Thinly slice the spring onions, adding the white parts to the cream and reserving the green parts for garnish. Cover and chill the dressing until needed.

Lift the steaks from the dish and cook over a high heat for 5 to 8 minutes on each side, depending on how well cooked you like your steak.

As soon as they are cooked, remove the steaks from the heat and leave to rest in a warm place for a few minutes before serving.

Serve with the dressing, garnished with the green spring onion tops.

Fillet Steaks with a Juniper Crust

Fillet steak is a real treat, but this recipe works equally well with other
cuts of steak, such as sirloin, rump or T-bone. The larger the surface area
of the meat, the more juniper mixture you will need.

Serves 6

- ❖ 30 ml/2 Tbsp dried
   juniper berries
- ❖ 10 ml/2 tsp black
   peppercorns

- ❖ 30 ml/2 Tbsp olive oil
- ❖ 10 ml/2 tsp Dijon mustard
- ❖ 5 ml/1 tsp salt
- ❖ 6 fillet steaks, about
   4 cm/1½ in thick

Grind the juniper berries and peppercorns to a powder in a grinder or using a pestle and mortar. Add the oil, mustard and salt and blend until smooth.

Rub the spice mixture over all surfaces of the steaks, cover and leave to stand for 1 to 2 hours.

Cook the fillets over a medium-high heat for about 4 to 6 minutes on each side, depending on how well done you like your steaks.

LEFT: TEXAN STEAKS WITH HORSERADISH DRESSING

Jerked Beef Kebabs

*The marinade for these kebabs is deeply flavoursome. Enjoy with a rice
dish or baked potatoes and a crisp side salad.*

Serves 6

❖ 45 ml/3 Tbsp olive oil
❖ 1 onion, roughly
    chopped
❖ 30 ml/2 Tbsp lemon juice
❖ 25 ml/1½ Tbsp dried
    thyme
❖ 25 ml/1½ Tbsp ground
    cinnamon
❖ 25 ml/1½ Tbsp caster
    sugar
❖ 15 ml/1 Tbsp chilli sauce

❖ 7.5 ml/1½ tsp
    ground
    coriander
❖ 7.5 ml/1½ tsp
    grated
    nutmeg
❖ 5 ml/1 tsp salt
❖ 5 ml/1 tsp ground black
    pepper
❖ 900 g/2 lb blade, sirloin
    or rump steak, cut into
    4 cm/1½ in cubes

Put all the ingredients, except the steak, into a blender or food processor and whiz until smooth. Tip into a large, shallow non-metallic dish.

Add the steak, stirring until well coated. Cover and leave to marinate for 2 hours or chilled for longer, stirring occasionally.

Thread the steak on to six flat metal skewers then cook over a medium-high heat for 6 to 8 minutes, turning occasionally, until cooked to your liking.

Tip

Instead of using a dish, put the meat and marinade into a strong plastic food bag and tie the opening. This makes it easy to squeeze the bag occasionally, moving the marinade around and making sure that every cube of steak is well coated.

RIGHT: JERKED BEEF KEBABS

Teriyaki Steaks

*This recipe calls for sake, Japanese rice wine, to be totally authentic.
However, a good fino sherry will serve just as well.*

Serves 6

❖ 45 ml/3 Tbsp Teriyaki
    sauce
❖ 45 ml/3 Tbsp lemon juice
❖ 30 ml/2 Tbsp rice vinegar
❖ 30 ml/2 Tbsp sake or dry
    sherry

❖ 7.5 cm/3 in piece of fresh
    root ginger
❖ 6 sirloin or rump
    steaks, about
    2 cm/¾ in thick

Put the first four ingredients into a large, shallow non-metallic dish.

Roughly grate the ginger, with its skin. Take the gratings in one hand and, with the dish beneath, squeeze until the juice runs through your fingers. Squeeze out as much as

you can. Discard the remaining pulp.

Add the steaks and turn them over in the mixture until well coated. Cover and leave to marinate for up to 2 hours.

Transfer the steaks to the barbecue and cook over a medium-high heat for 5 to 8 minutes on each side, depending on how well done you like them.

Tip

If time is short, it is not essential to leave these steaks to marinate. Just brush plenty of the Teriyaki mixture over and get cooking!

Burgers with Blue Cheese Dressing

Use any blue cheese you like for this dish, such as Stilton, Roquefort or
Danish Blue. They will all taste equally wonderful.

Serves 4

❖ 675 g/1½ lb minced
  lean beef
❖ 30 ml/2 Tbsp
  Worcestershire sauce
❖ Salt and ground black
  pepper

❖ 115 g/4 oz blue cheese
❖ 115 g/4 oz cream cheese
❖ 30 ml/2 Tbsp snipped
  fresh chives
❖ Olive oil, for brushing

Mix together the beef and Worcestershire sauce, seasoning the mixture well with salt and pepper. Shape into four burgers, cover and chill for 1 hour.

For the cheese dressing, put the cheeses and chives into a bowl and season with pepper. Blend with a fork. Cover and chill until needed.

Brush each of the burgers with olive oil. Cook over a medium-high heat for 5 to 7 minutes on each side, depending on how well you like your burgers cooked.

Serve each burger topped with a spoonful of the dressing.

Souvlaki

*These Greek pork kebabs are good served with a salad of ripe tomatoes
and a scattering of black olives.*

Serves 6

- ❖ 45 ml/3 Tbsp olive oil
- ❖ 2 plump garlic cloves, crushed
- ❖ 15 ml/1 Tbsp red wine vinegar
- ❖ 45 ml/3 Tbsp chopped fresh basil
- ❖ 25 ml/1½ Tbsp dried thyme
- ❖ 25 ml/1½ Tbsp dried oregano
- ❖ Salt and ground black pepper
- ❖ 800 g/1¾ lb lean pork, cut into cubes

Put all the ingredients except the pork into a large dish and whisk. Add the pork and stir until well coated. Cover and leave to marinate in the fridge for about 2 hours, stirring occasionally.

Thread the pork on to flat metal skewers and brush with any remaining marinade.

Cook over a medium heat for about 20 minutes, turning occasionally, or until they are cooked through.

Cajun Sticky Ribs

These delightfully gooey ribs may be served as a starter too. These quantities would easily serve eight people.

Serves 4

⬧ 2 kg/4 lb Chinese-style pork ribs

For the paste
⬧ 1 onion, roughly chopped
⬧ 3–4 plump garlic cloves
⬧ 1 red pepper, seeds removed and roughly chopped

⬧ 1 fresh red chilli
⬧ 75 ml/5 Tbsp black treacle
⬧ 30 ml/2 Tbsp red wine vinegar
⬧ 45 ml/3 Tbsp mixed dried herbs
⬧ Salt and ground black pepper

These ribs are best started off in the oven. Preheat the oven to 190°C/375°F/Gas Mark 5.

Arrange the ribs in a large roasting tin and cook for about 45 minutes, or until just tender. Transfer the ribs to a non-metallic dish, pouring off any excess fat.

Put the paste ingredients into a blender or food processor and whiz until almost smooth. Pour the mixture on to the ribs and brush it over to make sure they are all evenly coated. Cover the dish and leave the ribs to cool, turning and brushing them with the paste occasionally, until you are ready to cook them over the barbecue. (Once cooled, they should be chilled if you need to leave them for more than an hour before cooking.)

Once you are ready to cook, lift the ribs out of the marinade and cook on the barbecue over a medium-high heat for about 15 minutes, turning occasionally and basting with the remaining marinade, until brown and crisp or however you prefer them cooked.

Tip
When buying ribs, choose really meaty ones. Also, buying them in racks, rather than as individual ribs, makes them easier to turn on the barbecue. Precooking them in the oven ensures that they are tender before they go on to the barbecue.

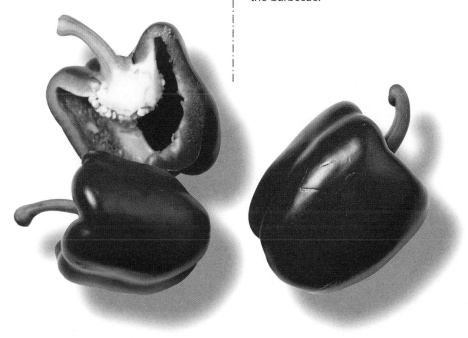

LEFT: CAJUN STICKY RIBS

Pork Stifado in Foil

*Based on a traditional Greek dish, the pork is cooked in foil on the
barbecue instead of in a pot.*

Serves 4

❖ 30 ml/2 Tbsp olive oil,
  plus extra for brushing
❖ 1 medium onion, thickly
  sliced
❖ 4 lean pork chops, each
  weighing about 225 g/
  8 oz
❖ Salt and freshly ground

black pepper
❖ 2 plump garlic cloves,
  finely chopped
❖ 4 medium tomatoes,
  sliced
❖ Ground allspice or cloves
❖ 4 sprigs of fresh thyme
❖ 30 ml/2 Tbsp red wine
  vinegar

Cut four large squares of thick foil, each large enough to make a loose parcel around a pork chop. Brush each square lightly with olive oil.

Lay one quarter of the onion on each piece of foil and place a pork chop on top. Season with salt and pepper, scatter the garlic over and add the tomato slices. Into each parcel, sprinkle a pinch of allspice and add a sprig of thyme. Drizzle over the remaining 2 tablespoons oil and the vinegar.

Fold the foil over and seal the parcels well.

Cook over low-to-medium heat for about 30 to 40 minutes, turning occasionally, until the pork and onions are tender and golden brown.

LEFT: PORK STIFADO IN FOIL

Oriental Glazed Pork

*Best cooked on a covered barbecue, this recipe is equally good using thick
pork loin chops instead of the whole loin.*

Serves 8

❖ 1.5 kg/3 lb loin of pork,
  chined (see Tip, below)
❖ 15 ml/1 Tbsp rice or
  white wine vinegar
❖ 15 ml/1 Tbsp light soy
  sauce

❖ 5 cm/2 in piece fresh
  root ginger, finely
  chopped
❖ 1.25 ml/¼ tsp Chinese
  five-spice powder
❖ Ground black pepper
❖ 60 ml/4 Tbsp clear honey
❖ 15 ml/1 Tbsp dry sherry

Using a very sharp knife, carefully remove the skin from the chined loin. Make several cuts through the fat side of the meat, almost through to the bone (it should look like eight chops linked together by the bones at the back of the joint).

Mix together the vinegar, soy sauce, ginger, Chinese five-spice powder and pepper, and rub the mixture over all surfaces of the pork. Cover and leave to marinate in the fridge for 1 hour or longer.

Cook, covered, over a medium heat for about 40 minutes, turning frequently, until almost cooked through.

Mix together the honey and sherry. Uncover the barbecue and brush the pork with the honey mixture. Continue cooking for 10 minutes, turning occasionally and brushing frequently with the glaze, or until glossy brown and cooked through.

Tip
Choose a pork loin with only a thin layer of fat. Ask your butcher to chine it (remove the backbone) for you.

Grilled Creole Combo Skewers

Seafood, steak and chicken unite to make wonderful kebabs, brushed with a pungent,
spicy seasoning before being barbecued to tender perfection.

Serves 4

- ❖ 8 headless raw tiger prawns
- ❖ 225 g/8 oz sirloin or rump steak, cut into 2.5 cm/ 1 in cubes
- ❖ 225 g/8 oz boneless, skinless chicken breast, cut into 2.5 cm/1 in cubes
- ❖ 225 g/8 oz monkfish, cut into 2.5 cm/1 in cubes

- ❖ 45 ml/3 Tbsp olive oil
- ❖ 5–10 ml/1–2 tsp chilli oil
- ❖ 15 ml/1 Tbsp lemon juice
- ❖ 5 ml/1 tsp Worcestershire sauce
- ❖ 4 spring onions, finely chopped
- ❖ 1 plump garlic clove, crushed
- ❖ 1 small celery stick, finely chopped
- ❖ Finely grated rind of ½ a lemon

Peel the prawns, leaving the tails intact. Divide the prawns, steak, chicken and monkfish into four portions and thread each portion on to a flat metal skewer.

Mix the remaining ingredients together and brush the mixture over the kebabs. Leave to stand for 10 minutes then brush again.

Transfer to the barbecue and cook over a medium-high heat for about 8 to 10 minutes, turning occasionally, or until the prawns and chicken are cooked through and the steak and fish are just tender. Serve immediately.

Skewered Venison with Tropical Fruits

Venison is now widely available from supermarkets as well as butchers. It is a very rich meat, and here is combined with prunes, mango and papaya.

Serves 4

- 675 g/1½ lb venison, preferably cut from the fillet
- 60 ml/4 Tbsp olive oil
- 1 small onion, finely chopped
- 4 whole cloves
- 1 cinnamon stick
- 4 ready-to-eat dried prunes, finely chopped
- 1 lemon
- Salt and ground black pepper
- 1 small ripe mango
- 1 small ripe papaya

Cut the venison into 4 centimetre/1½ inch cubes. Put the oil into a shallow non-metallic dish and add the onion, cloves, cinnamon and prunes. Pare the yellow rind from the lemon and add the strips to the oil mixture. Now squeeze the juice from the lemon and stir in. Season with salt and pepper.

Add the venison cubes to the dish, stirring until well coated. Cover and leave to marinate in the fridge for about 2 hours, stirring occasionally.

Peel the mango and cut the fruit off the stone in chunks. Halve the papaya and remove the seeds, then peel and cut the fruit into chunks.

Lift the venison out of the marinade and thread it on to metal skewers.

Cook over a medium-high heat for 10 minutes, turning occasionally and adding chunks of fruit to the ends of the skewers for the final 2 to 3 minutes.

Indonesian Pork Brochettes

Coconut, ginger, chillies and lime give a distinctly oriental flavour to these pork skewers. You could use cubed chicken instead if you prefer.

Serves 6

- 225 ml/8 fl oz coconut milk
- 6 spring onions
- 2 plump garlic cloves
- 2 fresh red chillies, halved and seeds removed
- 5 cm/2 in piece fresh root ginger, peeled and roughly chopped
- Finely grated rind and juice of 2 small limes
- 5 ml/1 tsp salt
- 5 ml/1 tsp ground black pepper
- Good pinch of ground turmeric
- 800 g/1¾ lb lean pork, cut into cubes
- Lime wedges, to serve

Put all the ingredients except the pork and lime wedges into a blender or food processor and whiz until the mixture is almost smooth.

Put the pork into a large non-metallic dish and pour the prepared coconut mixture over. Stir to coat well. Cover and leave to marinate in the fridge for about 2 hours, stirring occasionally.

Thread the pork cubes on to six flat metal skewers and brush with any remaining coconut mixture. Then cook over a medium heat for about 20 minutes, turning frequently, until cooked through. Serve with lime wedges for squeezing over.

Tip
For a fiery kick, leave the seeds in the chillies.

Chapter

6

Vegeta

ble Dishes

Corn on the Cob with Shallot and Herb Butter

Blackened Courgette and Sweet Onion Brochettes

Grilled Aubergine with Mozzarella Cheese and Tomato

Grilled Vegetable Platter

Roasted Wrapped Baby Vegetables

Squash Parcels with Brown Sugar

Vegetable and Sourdough Kebabs

Chinese Vegetable Stir Fry

Potato and Onion Grills with Olives

Spicy Pan-Fried Potatoes

Roasted Sweet Potatoes with Herb and Cinnamon Butter

Herbed Polenta with Wild Mushrooms

Stuffed Peppers

Baked Butternut Squash with Sweetcorn and Dill

Barbecued Baked Beans with Chilli

Kidney Bean Burgers with Pepper and Tomato

Corn on the Cob with Shallot and Herb Butter

*Sweetcorn is available in the summer and early autumn and so is a natural choice for the barbecue.
Choose medium-size cobs with their husks wrapped tightly around them.*

Serves 4

* 4 corn on the cob
* 115 g/4 oz soft butter
* 4 shallots, thinly sliced
  into rings
* 30 ml/2 Tbsp chopped

fresh parsley
* 4 sprigs of rosemary,
  each about 16 cm/5 in
  long
* Salt and ground black
  pepper

Place each cob on a sheet of thick foil. Thickly spread
one-quarter of the butter along the top of each. Scatter
the shallots and parsley over the top and add a sprig of
rosemary. Season lightly with salt and pepper.

Close the parcels, securing the seams well, then cook over
a medium heat for about 30 minutes, turning occasionally,
until the corn is tender and slightly scorched in places.

Serve in the parcels so each person can enjoy the herb
butter with the corn.

Blackened Courgette and Sweet Onion Brochettes

*The seasoning caramelizes a little during cooking, giving the vegetables a
slightly sweet accent which is totally delicious.*

Serves 6

✧ 45 ml/3 Tbsp olive oil
✧ 45 ml/3 Tbsp tomato purée
✧ 45 ml/3 Tbsp finely chopped fresh rosemary
✧ 15 ml/1 Tbsp caster sugar
✧ 24 small onions, peeled
✧ 6 courgettes, each cut into 4 pieces

Blend together the oil, tomato purée, rosemary and sugar.

Put the onions and the courgettes into a large, strong, plastic food bag and add the tomato mixture. Seal the opening and shake well until the vegetables are evenly coated. You can leave them in the bag until you are ready to cook.

Thread the onions and courgettes alternately on to six flat metal skewers.

Cook over a medium-high heat for about 15 minutes, turning occasionally, until slightly blackened and just cooked through.

Grilled Aubergine with Mozzarella Cheese and Tomato

These delightful aubergine parcels bring a taste of Italy to the barbecue,
with a top accent of fresh basil. Good served as a starter.

Serves 8

- ❖ 1 large aubergine, weighing about 450 g/1 lb
- ❖ Olive oil, for brushing
- ❖ 225 g/8 oz mozzarella cheese
- ❖ 2 large tomatoes
- ❖ Salt and ground black pepper
- ❖ 8 sprigs of basil

Trim the stalk off the aubergine and cut lengthways into 8 slices, each about 5 millimetres/¼ inch thick, discarding the ends. Lightly brush both sides of each slice with olive oil. Slice the cheese into 8 pieces. Cut the tomatoes into 8 slices, discarding the tops.

Cook one side of the aubergine slices over a medium-high heat for about 3 minutes until lightly charred and soft.

Lift off the grill on to a large plate, grilled sides up. Season lightly with salt and pepper. On to one end of each slice, place a slice of cheese, then a slice of tomato and top with a sprig of basil. Fold the aubergine over to make a parcel. Secure with a small, presoaked wooden skewer.

Cook over a medium-high heat for 3 to 4 minutes, turning once, until lightly charred. Serve immediately.

Grilled Vegetable Platter

This mixed vegetable dish is a meal in itself and ideal to serve if you are
catering for vegetarians as well as meat eaters.

Serves 6

- 90 ml/6 Tbsp olive oil
- 30 ml/2 Tbsp balsamic vinegar
- 30 ml/2 Tbsp fresh thyme leaves
- 1 large red onion, sliced into 6 rounds

- 12 baby beetroot, stems trimmed to 2.5 cm/1 in, peeled and halved lengthways
- 3 small courgettes, quartered lengthways
- 3 baby aubergines, quartered lengthways
- 2 red peppers, seeds removed and cut into 2.5 cm/1 in wide strips
- Salt and ground black pepper
- 60 ml/4 Tbsp freshly grated Parmesan cheese
- 30 ml/2 Tbsp chopped fresh parsley

Put the oil, vinegar and thyme into a large bowl and whisk lightly. Add the onion and beetroot and toss well. With a slotted spoon, lift them out and spread in a hinged wire rack. Add the remaining vegetables to the bowl and toss well. Use the slotted spoon to lift them out into a second hinged wire rack. Lightly season both sets of vegetables with salt and pepper.

Cook over a medium-high heat, turning occasionally. Allow the onion mixture about 8 to 10 minutes on each side and the courgette mixture about 6 minutes on each side until just cooked through.

Tip the vegetables on to a warmed platter and sprinkle with the Parmesan and parsley. Serve immediately.

Roasted Wrapped Baby Vegetables

Pesto and sun-dried tomatoes give a delicious kick to a lovely combination of tiny vegetables cooked in foil parcels.

Serves 4

- ◈ Butter, for greasing
- ◈ 450 g/1 lb mixed small vegetables, such as sugar-snap peas or mange-touts, asparagus tips, cherry tomatoes, baby sweetcorn and baby squash
- ◈ 1 small lime, cut into four wedges
- ◈ 30 ml/2 Tbsp pesto sauce

- ◈ 30 ml/2 Tbsp dry white wine
- ◈ 2 sun-dried tomatoes in oil, drained and cut into thin strips
- ◈ Ground black pepper

Grease four large squares of thick foil with butter and divide the vegetables

equally among them. Add a lime wedge to each.

Stir together the pesto, wine and tomatoes. Season with pepper then drizzle the mixture over the vegetables.

Close the parcels, securing the seams well. Cook over a medium heat for 8 to 10 minutes, turning the parcels at least once. The vegetables should still be slightly crisp.

Tip
Use scissors to snip the sun-dried tomatoes into strips.

Squash Parcels with Brown Sugar

Wedges of acorn squash are baked in foil, with butter and brown sugar enhancing the natural sweet flavour and luscious texture of the vegetable.

Serves 6

- ◈ 1 small acorn squash
- ◈ 115 g/4 oz butter
- ◈ 30 ml/6 tsp soft brown sugar

- ◈ Juice of 1 lemon
- ◈ Salt and ground black pepper
- ◈ 45 ml/3 Tbsp finely chopped fresh parsley

Halve the squash lengthways. Scoop out and discard the seeds and membranes. Cut each half lengthways into 3 wedges.

Put each wedge on a large sheet of thick foil and top with a portion of the butter and 5 millilitres/1 teaspoon sugar. Sprinkle with lemon juice, season with salt and black pepper and scatter over the parsley.

Close the parcels, securing the seams well. Cook over a medium heat for about 40 minutes, turning frequently, or until the squash is tender.

RIGHT: SQUASH PARCELS WITH BROWN SUGAR

Vegetable and Sourdough Kebabs

*The different textures of the vegetables and sourdough bread create an
interesting combination, and the bread doesn't even have to be absolutely fresh.*

Serves 6

- 2 courgettes, cut into 1 cm/½ in slices
- 12 closed-cup mushrooms
- 1 red pepper, seeds removed and cut into 12 even-size pieces
- Twelve 2.5 cm/1 in cubes sourdough bread

For the dressing

- 175 ml/6 fl oz olive oil
- 60 ml/4 Tbsp balsamic vinegar
- 4 shallots, roughly chopped
- 4 sun-dried tomatoes in oil, drained and roughly chopped
- 1 plump garlic clove
- 45 ml/3 Tbsp roughly chopped fresh parsley

LEFT: VEGETABLE AND SOURDOUGH KEBABS

Thread the vegetables and bread on to 6 long skewers. Lay them in a shallow dish or on a tray, large enough to hold them in a single layer.

Put the dressing ingredients into a blender or food processor and whiz until almost smooth. Brush the mixture over the kebabs, coating them well. Cover and leave to stand for 30 minutes to 1 hour. Lift the kebabs on to the barbecue and cook over a medium-high heat for about 10 minutes, turning occasionally and brushing with any remaining dressing.

Tip
If you do not have any sourdough bread, use a few thick slices of French bread, cut into quarters, instead.

Chinese Vegetable Stir Fry

*Cooking in a wok on the barbecue is great fun.
Impress your friends with this stir fry.*

Serves 6

- 125 ml/4 fl oz orange juice
- 45 ml/3 Tbsp light soy sauce
- 10 ml/2 tsp cornflour
- 5 ml/1 tsp sugar
- 30 ml/2 Tbsp vegetable oil
- 225 g/8 oz small whole green beans
- 4 medium carrots, thinly sliced
- Half a head of Chinese leaves, cut into large chunks
- 225 g/8 oz mange-tout
- 1 bunch of spring onions, thickly sliced
- 55 g/2 oz cashew nuts
- 15–30 ml/1–2 Tbsp sesame oil

Mix the orange juice with the soy sauce, then whisk in the cornflour and sugar.

Heat the vegetable oil in a large wok, add the beans and cook over high heat for 3 to 4 minutes, stirring. Add the carrots and Chinese leaves and cook, stirring for another 2 to 3 minutes. Add the mange-tout, spring onions and nuts and cook, stirring for a further 1 minute.

Whisk the orange mixture until it is well mixed, then add it to the wok, turning the vegetables so that they become coated with a thin layer of glossy sauce.

Sprinkle the sesame oil over and serve immediately.

Potato and Onion Grills
with Olives

*These potato parcels make a welcome change from the ubiquitous baked
potato that seems to be the usual barbecue fare.*

Serves 6

- ❖ 675 g/1½ lb potatoes,
  thinly sliced
- ❖ 1 large onion, thinly
  sliced
- ❖ 45 ml/3 Tbsp olive oil
- ❖ 15 ml/1 Tbsp white wine
  vinegar

- ❖ 45 ml/3 Tbsp fresh thyme
  leaves, or finely
  chopped fresh rosemary
- ❖ Salt and ground black
  pepper
- ❖ 16 stoned black olives

Put the potatoes and onion into a large bowl. Whisk
together the oil and vinegar, drizzle over the potato

mixture and toss well. Add the thyme or
rosemary, season with salt and pepper,
then toss again until evenly coated.

Divide the mixture among six large squares of thick
foil. Slice the olives into thin rings and scatter them
over the top.

Close the parcels, securing the seams well. Cook over a
medium heat for about 30 minutes, turning the parcels
occasionally, or until the potatoes are tender.

Spicy Pan-fried Potatoes

Serve these lightly-spiced potatoes with a dressing of thick Greek yoghurt or crème fraîche, seasoned with black pepper and chopped fresh coriander or mint.

Serves 6

- ❖ 30 ml/2 Tbsp olive oil
- ❖ 5 ml/1 tsp mustard seeds
- ❖ 5 ml/1 tsp fennel seeds
- ❖ 15 ml/1 Tbsp medium curry powder
- ❖ 675 g/1½ lb small new potatoes, cooked
- ❖ Chopped fresh coriander, to serve

Put the oil in a large frying pan or wok and heat up over medium coals.

Stir in the mustard seeds. When they begin to spit and pop, stir in the fennel seeds and curry powder.

Add the potatoes, shaking the pan to coat them with the spices. Cook over medium heat for about 10 minutes, stirring occasionally, or until the potatoes are golden brown all over.

Just before serving, sprinkle with fresh coriander.

Tip

This dish is just as good when made with drained, canned new potatoes.

Roasted Sweet Potatoes with Herb and Cinnamon Butter

Sweet potatoes come in two basic varieties: the pale yellow, dryish type and the orangey moist sort. Choose the latter out of preference although either may be used in this dish.

Serves 4

- ❖ 675 g/1½ lb sweet potato, peeled and thinly sliced
- ❖ 15 ml/1 Tbsp lemon juice
- ❖ 55 g/2 oz soft butter
- ❖ 60 ml/4 Tbsp finely chopped fresh parsley
- ❖ 20 ml/4 tsp soft brown sugar
- ❖ 2.5 ml/½ tsp ground cinnamon

Put the sweet potato slices into a plastic food bag and add the lemon juice. Seal the opening and shake until well coated. This will prevent the potato turning brown.

Divide the prepared sweet potato mixture among four large squares of thick foil.

Mix together the remaining ingredients. Add one-quarter of the mixture to each parcel then close the parcels, securing the seams well.

Cook over a medium heat for about 30 minutes, turning the parcels occasionally, or until the sweet potato is tender.

Herbed Polenta with Wild Mushrooms

If you cannot find wild mushrooms used common cultivated ones instead but make sure they are closed cup rather than open cup or flat or the sauce will turn an unappetizing grey colour.

This dish is also delicious served with prosciutto, snipped into strips and scattered over, or stirred into, the mushroom topping.

Serves 6

- ❖ **225 g/8 oz instant polenta**
- ❖ **2.5 ml/½ tsp salt**
- ❖ **85 g/3 oz butter**
- ❖ **30 ml/2 Tbsp dried oregano, thyme or a mixture**
- ❖ **55 g/2 oz finely grated Parmesan cheese**
- ❖ **30 ml/2 Tbsp olive oil, plus extra for brushing**
- ❖ **175 g/6 oz shallots, thinly sliced**
- ❖ **2 plump garlic cloves, very thinly sliced**
- ❖ **550 g/1¼ lb mixed fresh mushrooms, such as field, oyster and shiitake, cleaned and sliced (see Tip, below)**
- ❖ **125 ml/4 fl oz dry white wine**
- ❖ **Salt and ground black pepper**
- ❖ **45 ml/3 Tbsp double cream**
- ❖ **Chopped fresh parsley or coriander**

In a large pan, bring 1.2 litres/2 pints water to the boil. Add the polenta and salt, stirring briskly, until the mixture becomes thick and smooth.

Remove from the heat and stir in 55 grams/2 ounces of the butter, the herbs and the Parmesan. Tip the mixture into an oiled shallow dish or tin, measuring about 20 centimetres/8 inches square. Leave to cool completely.

Cut the polenta into six rectangles and brush the two large sides of each with olive oil. Cook over a medium-high heat for 4 to 5 minutes on each side, or until crisp, brown and heated through.

Meanwhile, in a large pan, heat the olive oil and the remaining butter. Add the shallots and garlic and cook over a medium heat for about 5 minutes, stirring frequently, until soft but not brown.

Add the mushrooms and cook over a high heat for 2 to 3 minutes, stirring once or twice. Pour in the wine and heat until bubbling. Season to taste with salt and pepper, then stir in the cream.

To serve, spoon the mushrooms on top of the grilled polenta. Scatter over some chopped parsley or coriander.

Tip

Wild mushrooms usually contain some sand and may be harbouring insects. To prepare them, trim off and discard any tough stems, then either wash under cold running water or, if they are very delicate, wipe carefully with a dampened piece of kitchen paper. Make sure they are dry before adding to the dish.

RIGHT: HERBED POLENTA WITH WILD MUSHROOMS

Stuffed Peppers

Red or yellow peppers create a natural 'basket' for other vegetables and chopped ham, and impart a lovely, slightly sweet flavour to each bite.

Serves 4

- ❖ 2 large red or yellow peppers
- ❖ 30 ml/2 Tbsp olive oil
- ❖ 1 small onion, finely chopped
- ❖ 2 plump garlic cloves, finely chopped
- ❖ 1 small aubergine, weighing about 225 g/ 8 oz, chopped
- ❖ 1 large courgette, chopped

- ❖ 45 ml/3 Tbsp tomato purée
- ❖ 45 ml/3 Tbsp dry white wine
- ❖ Salt and ground black pepper
- ❖ 55 g/2 oz smoked ham, finely chopped
- ❖ 20 ml/4 tsp finely chopped fresh parsley
- ❖ 20 ml/4 tsp finely grated Parmesan cheese

Halve the peppers lengthways, cutting through the stem. Remove and discard all seeds.

Heat the oil in a pan. Add the onion and garlic and cook over a medium heat for about 5 minutes, stirring

LEFT: STUFFED PEPPERS

frequently, until soft but not brown. Stir in the aubergine and courgette. Cook over a medium heat until the vegetables are tender.

Stir the tomato purée into the wine and add to the vegetables. Season to taste with salt and pepper. Remove from the heat and stir in the ham.

Fill the pepper halves with the vegetable mixture, pressing it in firmly. Arrange them, cut side down, on four oiled squares of thick foil.

Cook, foil side down, over a medium heat for about 5 minutes or until the surface of the stuffing is lightly browned. Turn the peppers over and continue cooking for about 10 to 15 minutes until the peppers are soft and slightly charred. Carefully remove the foil. Mix together the parsley and Parmesan and scatter over the peppers. Serve immediately.

Tip
For a spicy flavour, use chilli oil instead of the olive oil.

Baked Butternut Squash with Sweetcorn and Dill

The creamy consistency of the squash contrasts well with the crisp bite of sweetcorn in these delectable vegetable parcels.

Serves 4

- ❖ 1 butternut squash, weighing about 550 g/1¼ lb, halved, seeds removed, peeled and cut into 2 cm/¾ in dice
- ❖ 115 g/4 oz sweetcorn

- ❖ 55 g/2 oz soft butter
- ❖ 45 ml/3 Tbsp chopped fresh dill
- ❖ 25 ml/1½ Tbsp snipped fresh chives
- ❖ Salt and ground black pepper
- ❖ 60 ml/4 Tbsp white wine

Divide the squash among four large squares of foil. Add one-quarter of the sweetcorn to each. Blend the butter, dill, chives and seasoning. Top each parcel with one-quarter of the butter mixture and add 15 millilitres/ 1 tablespoon wine to each.

Close the parcels, securing the seams well, then cook over a medium heat for 25 to 30 minutes, turning occasionally, until they are tender.

Barbecued Baked Beans with Chilli

Home-made baked beans could not be more different from the commercial varieties. Once you have tasted these, you will never buy another can.

Serves 8

- 15 ml/1 Tbsp oil
- 4 lean bacon rashers, finely chopped
- 1 onion, thinly sliced into rings
- 1 red pepper, seeds removed and cut into 1 cm/½ in dice
- 1 green pepper, seeds removed and cut into 1 cm/½ in dice
- 300 ml/½ pt tomato ketchup
- 60 ml/4 Tbsp black treacle
- 45 ml/3 Tbsp wholegrain mustard
- 15 ml/1 Tbsp white wine vinegar
- 15 ml/1 Tbsp chilli sauce, or to taste
- 550 g/1¼ lb cooked haricot or cannellini beans
- Salt and ground black pepper

Put the oil into a large pan and add the bacon and onion. Cook over a medium heat, stirring frequently, until the onion is soft but not brown.

Add the peppers and cook for about 2 minutes, stirring once or twice.

Mix together the ketchup, treacle, mustard, vinegar and chilli sauce. Stir the mixture into the vegetables.

Add the beans to the pan. Bring to the boil, then simmer gently over a low heat (or on the side of the barbecue), stirring occasionally, for about 15 minutes.

Kidney Bean Burgers with Pepper and Tomato

Serve these burgers as they are, with plenty of crisp salad, or in a flat roll, split and toasted on the side of the barbecue, with a sliced tomato and lettuce garnish.

Serves 8

- 60 ml/4 Tbsp olive oil, plus extra for brushing
- 1 large carrot, finely chopped
- 1 large onion, finely chopped
- 3 plump garlic cloves, finely chopped
- 2 red peppers, seeds removed and finely chopped
- 6 fresh tomatoes, skinned, seeds removed and finely chopped
- 30 ml/2 Tbsp fresh oregano
- Two 400g/14 oz cans red kidney beans, drained
- 175 g/6 oz fresh breadcrumbs
- 120 ml/8 Tbsp chopped fresh parsley
- 2 eggs
- 60 ml/4 Tbsp tomato ketchup
- Salt and ground black pepper

Heat the oil in a large pan and add the carrot, onion, garlic and peppers. Cook over a medium heat for about 15 minutes, stirring occasionally. Stir in the tomatoes and oregano. Tip into a large bowl and leave until cold.

Tip the beans into a food processor and whiz until smooth. Add the beans, breadcrumbs and parsley to the bowl. Lightly beat the eggs with the tomato ketchup or purée and add to the bowl. Season with salt and pepper. Divide the mixture into eight and shape each one into a burger. Cover and chill for at least 2 hours.

Brush the burgers with olive oil. Cook over a medium-high heat for about 7 minutes on each side. Serve immediately.

RIGHT: KIDNEY BEAN BURGERS WITH PEPPER AND TOMATO

Chapter

7

Salads,

Salsas and Breads

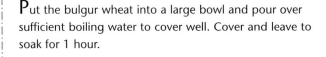

Tabbouleh with Mango

*Tabbouleh, which originated in Lebanon, traditionally has tomatoes in it.
Here diced mango is used instead to brilliant effect.*

Serves 8

- 350 g/12 oz bulgur wheat
- 2 mangoes, stones removed, peeled and diced
- 1 red onion, very thinly sliced
- ½ cucumber, halved

lengthways, seeds removed and sliced
- 90 ml/6 Tbsp finely chopped fresh parsley
- 45 ml/3 Tbsp finely chopped fresh mint
- 90 ml/6 Tbsp olive oil
- Juice of 2 large lemons
- Salt and ground black pepper

Put the bulgur wheat into a large bowl and pour over sufficient boiling water to cover well. Cover and leave to soak for 1 hour.

Put the remaining ingredients into a large bowl.

Drain the wheat, then tip into a clean dish towel and squeeze out any excess moisture. Add to the bowl with the rest of the ingredients and toss to mix well.

Cover and leave to stand for about 30 minutes before stirring and serving.

RIGHT: TABBOULEH WITH MANGO

Classic Coleslaw

*What barbecue party would be complete without a large
bowl of creamy coleslaw? It is so easy to make yet impressive too.*

Serves 8

- 900 g/2 lb white cabbage, trimmed and finely shredded
- 1 large carrot, grated
- 1 large onion, finely chopped
- 45 ml/3 Tbsp chopped fresh parsley
- 4 celery sticks, thinly sliced
- Salt and ground black pepper

- 200 ml/7 fl oz mayonnaise

Put the cabbage into a large bowl and add the carrot, onion, parsley and celery. Toss to mix.

Season the mayonnaise well with salt and pepper. Pour over the vegetable mixture and toss until evenly coated.

Cover and chill for 2 to 3 hours, to allow the flavours to mingle. Remove from the fridge about 30 minutes before serving at room temperature.

Tip
For a change, try replacing half the mayonnaise with thick yoghurt or soured cream.

Red Cabbage Coleslaw

*Here is a wonderfully colourful variation on the classic coleslaw, with an
added 'crunch' provided by the peanuts.*

Serves 8

- 350 g/12 oz red cabbage, very finely shredded
- 1 large carrot, grated
- 1 small onion, finely chopped
- 90 ml/6 Tbsp mayonnaise
- 5 ml/1 tsp caster sugar
- 45 ml/3 Tbsp soured cream
- 15 ml/1 Tbsp tomato ketchup
- 15 ml/1 Tbsp white wine vinegar
- 5 ml/1 tsp Worcestershire sauce
- 55 g/2 oz shelled peanuts

Put the cabbage into a large bowl. Add the carrot and onion and mix well.

Mix together the mayonnaise, soured cream, ketchup, vinegar, sugar and Worcestershire sauce. Spoon the mixture over the vegetables and toss until well coated. Cover and chill for 2 to 3 hours, to allow the flavours to mingle and develop.

Remove from the fridge about 30 minutes before serving. Serve at room temperature with the peanuts scattered over the top.

RIGHT: RED CABBAGE COLESLAW

Waldorf Salad

*This is a fresh-tasting crunchy salad which goes well
with grilled meats and fish.*

Serves 8

- 4 large crunchy eating apples, preferably with red skins
- Juice of half a lemon
- ½ tsp sugar
- 1 small head of celery, trimmed and sliced
- 85 g/3 oz walnut pieces
- 5 Tbsp mayonnaise
- 5 Tbsp Greek style yoghurt
- Salt and freshly ground black pepper

Halve the apples lengthways, remove their cores and cut into 1 centimetre/½ inch cubes.

In a large bowl, toss the apples in the lemon juice. Sprinkle the sugar over them and add the celery slices and the walnut pieces.

Stir together the mayonnaise and yoghurt and season to taste. Add to the apple mixture and toss until well coated.

Tip
This looks pretty when garnished with thin slices of apple (dipped in lemon juice to prevent them discolouring) and walnut halves.

Rice Salad with Feta Cheese Dressing

The cheese dressing is combined with the rice while it is still warm, along with the vegetables, so that the flavours are fully developed before serving.

Serves 8

- 450 g/1 lb long grain rice
- 90 ml/6 Tbsp corn or olive oil
- 45 ml/3 Tbsp red wine vinegar
- 10 ml/2 tsp Dijon mustard
- 10 ml/2 tsp caster sugar
- 30 ml/2 Tbsp chopped fresh herbs, such as oregano, thyme or rosemary
- 200 g/7 oz feta cheese, crumbled
- 1 red pepper, seeds removed and cut into small dice
- 1 green pepper, seeds removed and cut into small dice
- 115 g/4 oz cooked sweetcorn, canned or frozen
- 1 small red onion, finely chopped
- 6 spring onions, sliced

Cook the rice following the instructions on the packet. Drain, if necessary, tip into a large bowl and leave to stand while you make the dressing.

Put the oil into a bowl and add the vinegar, mustard, sugar and herbs. Whisk until blended. Stir in the crumbled cheese. Pour over the warm rice and stir well.

Add the remaining ingredients and toss well.

Cover and leave to stand for at least 30 minutes before tossing lightly and serving.

Couscous with Apricots and Pistachios

A staple of the North African diet, couscous, which is steamed semolina, combines delightfully with fruit and nuts in this attractive and delicious salad.

Serves 8

* 350 g/12 oz couscous (choose the precooked variety)
* 90 ml/6 Tbsp olive oil
* Finely grated rind and juice of 1 large lemon
* 15 ml/1 Tbsp Dijon mustard
* 10 ml/2 tsp caster sugar
* 115 g/4 oz ready-to-eat dried apricots, cut into very thin slivers
* 115 g/4 oz shelled pistachios, roughly chopped
* 30 ml/2 Tbsp chopped fresh parsley
* Several sprigs fresh basil, to garnish

Cook the couscous in plenty of boiling water for 3 to 5 minutes or until tender. Drain well and tip into a large bowl. Leave to stand while you make the dressing.

Whisk together the oil, lemon rind and juice, mustard and sugar. Pour over the warm couscous and stir well.

Leave to cool to room temperature, then stir in the apricots, pistachios and parsley. Cover and leave to stand until required.

Just before serving, tear the basil into shreds and scatter over the top of the salad.

Calypso Rice

There is a West Indian influence to this lovely salad which combines fruit and pine nuts with flavoursome brown rice.

Serves 8

* 350 g/12 oz brown rice
* 90 ml/6 Tbsp olive oil
* 45 ml/3 Tbsp cider vinegar
* 15 ml/1 Tbsp wholegrain mustard
* 10 ml/2 tsp soft brown sugar
* 30 ml/2 Tbsp chopped fresh coriander
* 8 spring onions, chopped
* 200 g/7 oz can pineapple in fruit juice, drained and chopped
* 1 papaya, halved, seeds removed, peeled and diced
* 115 g/4 oz pine nuts, toasted

Cook the rice, following the instructions on the packet. Drain, if necessary, and tip into a large bowl. Leave to stand while you make the dressing.

Whisk together the oil, vinegar, mustard and sugar. Pour over the warm rice and stir well.

Add the coriander, onion, pineapple and papaya, then toss well.

Cover and leave to stand for at least 30 minutes. Toss lightly, sprinkle with the pine nuts and serve.

Chilli Bean Salad

This substantial, hearty salad goes well with barbecued steaks, burgers and other meats.

Serves 8

- 45 ml/3 Tbsp olive oil
- 1 large onion, thinly sliced
- 2 plump garlic cloves, finely chopped
- 1 red pepper, seeds removed and finely diced
- 1 yellow pepper, seeds removed and finely diced
- 4 large ripe tomatoes, skinned and chopped
- 400 g/14 oz can haricot or cannellini beans, drained
- 400g/14 oz can red kidney or black beans, drained
- 45 ml/3 Tbsp chilli oil
- Juice of 1 lemon
- 15 ml/1 Tbsp clear honey
- Salt and ground black pepper
- 45 ml/3 Tbsp finely chopped fresh rosemary

Heat the olive oil in a large pan and add the onion, garlic and peppers. Cook gently for about 10 minutes, stirring occasionally, until the vegetables are very soft but not brown. Stir in the tomatoes and beans and heat, stirring frequently, until the mixture begins to bubble at the base of the pan. Then tip it into a large bowl.

Whisk together the chilli oil, lemon, honey and seasoning. Stir in the rosemary. Pour the dressing over the warm beans and stir well. Cover and leave to cool, stirring gently occasionally.

Serve at room temperature.

Pasta Salad with Caramelized Onion, Olives and Walnuts

Onions are cooked very, very slowly so that they become meltingly sweet and gooey. Then they are simply combined with pasta shapes, with black olives and walnuts added just before serving.

Serves 6

- 60 ml/4 Tbsp olive oil
- 2 large onions, halved lengthways and very thinly sliced
- 10 ml/2 tsp caster sugar
- 25 ml/1½ Tbsp tarragon, cider or white wine vinegar
- 225 g/8 oz pasta shapes, such as penne
- 115 g/4 oz stoned black olives, halved

- 115 g/4 oz walnut halves, lightly toasted and roughly chopped

Heat the oil in a large frying pan, add the onions and sprinkle with the sugar. Cook very gently for 30 to 40 minutes, stirring occasionally, until the onions are very soft, sweet and a rich golden brown. Leave to cool for about 10 minutes, then stir in the vinegar of your choice.

Meanwhile, cook the pasta in plenty of salted water, according to the instructions on the packet. Drain well and tip into a large bowl. Add the onions, scraping any juices and bits from the base of the pan. Toss lightly. Cover and leave to stand until ready to use.

Before serving, stir gently and scatter the olives and walnuts over. Serve at room temperature.

New Potato Salad with Creamy Dill Dressing

There is a Scandinavian touch to this potato salad in its use of soured cream and dill.
It would go well with barbecued fish, especially salmon.

Serves 8–10

- ❖ 1 kg/2¼ lb small new potatoes, scrubbed
- ❖ 150 ml/5 fl oz mayonnaise
- ❖ 150 ml/5 fl oz soured cream
- ❖ 15 ml/1 Tbsp lemon juice
- ❖ 60 ml/4 Tbsp chopped fresh dill
- ❖ Salt and ground black pepper
- ❖ 30 ml/2 Tbsp finely grated Parmesan cheese
- ❖ Sprigs of dill, to garnish

Cook the potatoes in boiling salted water until tender. Drain and put into a large bowl.

Mix together the mayonnaise, soured cream, lemon juice and chopped dill. Season to taste with salt and ground pepper.

While the potatoes are still warm, add the prepared mayonnaise mixture and stir gently to coat well. Cover and leave to cool.

Just before serving, stir gently. Scatter the Parmesan cheese over the top and garnish with dill.

Grilled Vegetable Salad

*Peppers, aubergine, courgette and tomatoes combine their delightful
flavours in this attractive salad.*

Serves 8

❖ 75 ml/5 Tbsp olive oil,
plus extra for brushing
❖ 15 ml/1 Tbsp balsamic or
red wine vinegar
❖ 10 ml/2 tsp caster sugar
❖ 2 red peppers, seeds
removed and cut into
4 cm/1½ in strips
❖ 2 yellow peppers, seeds
removed and cut into
4 cm/1½ in strips

❖ 1 large aubergine, cut
into 1 cm/½ in rings
❖ 4 large courgettes, stalks
removed and each sliced
lengthways into 4 strips
❖ 4 beefsteak tomatoes,
cut into 1 cm/½ in slices
❖ 30 ml/2 Tbsp fresh thyme
leaves
❖ Black olives, to serve

Whisk together the olive oil, vinegar and sugar. Set aside.

Lightly brush the vegetables with oil on all sides. Cook the peppers first, skin side down, over a medium-high heat until the skin is quite charred and beginning to lift away from the flesh. Quickly pop them into a plastic bag, seal the opening and leave to cool.

Cook the aubergine and courgettes until soft and slightly charred on both sides. Lift on to a serving platter.

Cook the tomatoes only lightly. Try to char the edges without completely cooking the flesh. If necessary, cook on one side only. Transfer to the platter.

Remove the peppers from the plastic bag, reserving any juices. Remove and discard the skins. Add the peppers to the other vegetables.

Add the reserved pepper juices to the dressing and drizzle over the vegetables. Sprinkle with the thyme and scatter over some black olives.

Mango and Red Onion Salsa

*The juice from fresh root ginger gives a warm yet delicate flavour to the
mangoes in this lovely, vibrant salsa.*

Serves 6

❖ 2 large ripe mangoes,
stones removed, peeled
and chopped
❖ 1 red onion, finely
chopped
❖ 5 ml/1 tsp finely grated
lime rind

❖ 30 ml/2 Tbsp lime juice
❖ 45 ml/3 Tbsp fresh root
ginger juice (see Tip,
opposite)
❖ Pinch of cayenne pepper
❖ 60 ml/4 Tbsp chopped
fresh coriander

Place all the ingredients together in a large bowl. Stir gently to mix well.

Chill the salsa for 1 hour before serving.

Tip
To make ginger juice, roughly grate a piece of fresh root ginger, without peeling it. Take a fistful of the gratings and, with a bowl beneath your hand, squeeze until the juice runs through your fingers. For 45 millilitres/ 3 tablespoons, you will need a fat 5 centimetre/2 inch long piece of ginger.

RIGHT: MANGO AND RED ONION SALSA

Two-tomato Salsa

This is a wonderfully sweet and rich salsa, combining tiny cherry with gutsy sun-dried
tomatoes. Olive oil and fresh basil are added for a truly authentic Mediterranean flavour.

Serves 6

⬧ 225 g/8 oz cherry
tomatoes, halved
⬧ 8 sun-dried tomatoes in
oil, drained and
chopped into small
pieces

⬧ 6 large spring onions,
thinly sliced
⬧ 30 ml/2 Tbsp olive oil
⬧ 30 ml/2 Tbsp balsamic
vinegar
⬧ 5 ml/1 tsp caster sugar
⬧ Handful of fresh basil
leaves

Put the two types of tomato into a large bowl and add the spring onions.

Whisk together the oil, vinegar and sugar. Pour over the tomatoes, toss to coat well then cover and chill for 1 hour.

Just before serving, tear the basil leaves into shreds and stir into the salsa.

Red Pepper and Black Olive Salsa

*Red pepper, black olives and bright green coriander combine to make an eye-catching
and deeply flavoured salsa. This salsa will complement any lamb,
pork or chicken dish prepared on the barbecue.*

Serves 6

- ❖ 2 red peppers, quartered lengthways and seeds removed
- ❖ 24 stoned black olives, sliced into rings
- ❖ 45 ml/3 Tbsp olive oil
- ❖ 1 large plump garlic clove, crushed
- ❖ Finely grated rind and juice of 1 lemon
- ❖ Handful of fresh coriander, roughly chopped

Put the peppers, skin side down, over a medium-high heat until the skin is quite charred and beginning to lift away from the flesh. Quickly pop them into a plastic bag, seal the opening and leave to cool.

Remove the cooled peppers from the bag, reserving any juices. Remove and discard the skins and cut the flesh into small dice or thin strips.

Put the peppers into a bowl and add the olive rings to them.

Whisk together the oil, garlic, lemon rind and juice and pour over the peppers. Stir gently to coat well then cover and chill for 1 hour.

Just before serving, stir in the coriander.

Guacamole

*This classic dish may be served as a nibble or starter, with vegetables and crisps for dipping,
or as an accompaniment to grilled food. It is especially good combined with salad leaves
and barbecued meat or poultry stuffed into warmed pitta bread.*

Serves 6

- ❖ 4 large ripe tomatoes, halved and seeds removed
- ❖ 1 small red onion, roughly chopped
- ❖ 1–3 fresh red chillies, depending on their strength, halved and seeds removed
- ❖ 2 plump garlic cloves
- ❖ 3 ripe avocados, halved, stones removed and skinned
- ❖ Juice of 2 limes
- ❖ 5 ml/1 tsp tomato purée
- ❖ Large handful of fresh coriander
- ❖ Salt and ground black pepper

Whiz the tomato halves, onion, chillies and garlic in a blender or food processor until they form a rough purée.

Add the avocado, lime juice, tomato purée, coriander and seasoning. Whiz again to make a rough mixture.

Spoon into a bowl and serve.

Tip

Guacamole can discolour quite quickly so should not be prepared very much ahead of time. If you do prepare it early, place some clear film over the surface of the mixture, excluding all the air, and this will help to prevent discolouration.

Garlic Bread

*Everyone likes garlic bread, so make sure you provide enough.
It is a great standby to have on hand for people to nibble while you are
cooking the main course on the barbecue.*

Serves 8

* 115 g/4 oz slightly salted butter
* 3 plump garlic cloves, crushed
* 45 ml/3 Tbsp chopped fresh parsley
* Ground black pepper
* 1 long thick French stick

Soften the butter and blend in the garlic, parsley and some pepper.

Cut the bread diagonally into thick slices, cutting nearly but not quite all the way through. Spread the garlic butter on both sides of each slice and re-assemble the loaf.

Wrap in thick foil, securing the seams well, then cook over a medium heat for about 10 minutes, turning occasionally, until crisp and hot.

Warm Tomato and Herb Bruschetta

*It does not matter if the bruschetta sit for a little while
once they have been put together. The tomato mixture soaks slightly into
the toasted bread, with delightful results.*

Serves 6 as a starter

* 675 g/1½ lb ripe tomatoes, preferably plum, peeled, seeds removed and chopped
* 2 plump garlic cloves, finely chopped
* Salt and ground black pepper
* 15 ml/1 Tbsp balsamic vinegar
* 15 ml/1 Tbsp extra virgin olive oil
* 5 ml/1 tsp lemon juice
* 6 slices crusty bread, about 2 cm/½ in thick
* 60 ml/4 Tbsp chopped fresh basil leaves

Put the tomatoes and garlic into a pan and season to taste with salt and pepper. Leave on the side of the barbecue to warm through gently.

Once the tomatoes are warm (not hot), stir in the vinegar, oil and lemon juice.

Toast the bread until golden brown on both sides. Lift on to serving plates.

Stir the basil into the tomato mixture, pile on top of the bread and serve.

Mediterranean Bread Rolls

*These flavoursome rolls may be eaten just as they are, or filled with
burgers or other delights from the barbecue.*

Serves 6

- ❖ **6 large bread rolls, such
  as ciabatta**
- ❖ **Olive oil, for drizzling**
- ❖ **6 sun-dried tomatoes,
  chopped**
- ❖ **18 stoned green olives,
  cut into quarters**
- ❖ **Handful of fresh basil
  leaves**
- ❖ **Ground black pepper**

Split the rolls horizontally and drizzle the cut surfaces
with olive oil.

Over the six bases, scatter the chopped tomatoes, olives,
some torn basil leaves and a sprinkling of black pepper.

Re-assemble the rolls, wrap securely in thick foil then cook
over a medium-high heat for about 10 minutes, turning
occasionally, or until the bread is toasted on the outside
and warm inside.

Tip
If you prefer, use a French stick, split lengthways and
filled. To serve, unwrap the foil and slice as required.

Chapter

8

Desse

rts

Nectarines with Orange and Almond Butter

*The delicate flavours of nectarines and almonds combine to create a light
dessert, just right for serving after a hearty mixed barbecue.*

Serves 6

- 3 ripe nectarines
- 1 large orange
- 1.25 ml/¼ tsp almond
  essence

- 55 g/2 oz butter
- Whipped cream or thick
  yoghurt, to serve
- 6 amaretti biscuits,
  crushed

Halve the nectarines and remove their stones. Stand each half, cut side up, on a large square of thick foil.

Using a vegetable peeler, pare the rind from half the orange and cut into very thin strips. Pour boiling water over the strips and stand for 10 minutes. Squeeze the juice from the orange and stir in the almond essence. Divide the butter into six pieces.

Into each nectarine half, put some of the orange juice, a piece of butter and some drained strips of orange rind. Then gather the foil like a pouch and squeeze to seal well.

Cook the parcels, seam side up, over a medium heat for about 10 minutes, until the fruit has softened slightly, is warmed through and the butter has melted.

Open the parcels and top the fruit with whipped cream or yoghurt and the crushed amaretti biscuits.

LEFT: NECTARINES WITH ORANGE AND ALMOND BUTTER

Lemon Baked Bananas with Citrus Mascarpone

*The dense flesh of bananas makes them an ideal choice for barbecuing.
The inclusion of mascarpone cheese makes this a very rich dessert.*

Serves 4

- 225 g/8 oz mascarpone
  cheese
- Finely grated rind and
  juice of 1 lemon
- Icing sugar, to taste

- 55 g/2 oz butter
- 55 g/2 oz soft brown
  sugar
- 4 large bananas
- 20 ml/4 tsp toasted
  chopped hazelnuts

Put the cheese into a bowl and blend in the lemon rind. Add icing sugar to taste, then cover and chill until needed.

Put the butter, brown sugar and lemon juice into a small pan and heat until melted.

Thickly slice the bananas and divide among four squares of thick foil. Pour the butter mixture over.

Close the parcels, securing the seams well then cook over a medium heat for about 10 minutes.

Serve immediately topped with the mascarpone mixture and sprinkled with the hazelnuts.

Warm Tropical Fruit Salad

This dessert is delicious served with a scoop of coconut ice cream.

Serves 4

* Butter, for greasing
* 1 ripe mango, stone removed, peeled and sliced
* 1 orange, peeled and cut into segments
* 1 papaya, halved, seeds removed, peeled and sliced
* 1 banana, peeled and thickly sliced
* 2 passion fruit
* 60 ml/4 Tbsp dark rum
* 20 ml/4 tsp dark soft brown sugar
* 1.25 ml/¼ tsp grated nutmeg
* 1.25 ml/¼ tsp ground cinnamon

Grease four large squares of thick foil. Divide the mango, orange, papaya and banana among them. Cut the passion fruit in half, scoop out the seeds and scatter them over the other fruit. Gather up the foil around the fruit.

Mix the remaining ingredients together until the sugar dissolves and spoon over the fruit.

Close the foil parcels, pouch style, then cook, seam side up, over a medium heat for about 5 minutes, or until warmed through.

Glazed Pineapple with Coconut Rum Cream

Strictly for the grown-ups! Make sure the children are occupied elsewhere
when you serve up this decadent dessert.

Serves 6

❖ 1 small pineapple, skin
   and core removed and
   cut into 2.5 cm/
   1 in thick slices
❖ 85 g/3 oz unsalted butter,
   melted

❖ Icing sugar, to taste
❖ 300 ml/½ pt double
   cream
❖ 10 ml/2 tsp coconut
   liqueur, such as Cocody
❖ 10 ml/2 tsp dark rum

Brush the pineapple on all sides with the melted butter.
Lightly dust with icing sugar. Put the cream into a bowl
and stir in icing sugar to taste. Add the liqueur and rum.

Lightly whip to smooth peaks. Cover and chill until required.

Cook the pineapple over a medium-high heat for 2 to
3 minutes on each side, until glazed and slightly scorched.
Serve with the flavoured cream.

Tip
If you cannot find coconut liqueur, simply use grated,
creamed coconut milk with a splash of brandy added
instead. The result will be just as delicious.

Warm Fruit and Marshmallow Kebabs with Chocolate Fondue

This is a fun dessert to produce at the end of a barbecue. Everyone dips into the chocolate sauce, and will probably require a paper napkin or two.

Serves 4

- ❖ 16 strawberries
- ❖ Wedge of watermelon, cut into 4 cm/1½ in cubes
- ❖ 16 marshmallows
- ❖ 175 g/6 oz plain chocolate
- ❖ 45 ml/3 Tbsp golden syrup
- ❖ 15 ml/1 Tbsp lemon juice

Thread the fruit pieces and the marshmallows on to eight small skewers.

Put the chocolate, syrup and lemon juice into a small flameproof dish. Heat gently, stirring frequently until melted, glossy and smooth. Move to the edge of the barbecue to keep them warm.

Cook the kebabs over a medium heat for a few minutes, turning once, until just warmed through.

Serve immediately with the chocolate sauce for dipping the kebabs into, fondue style.

RIGHT: WARM FRUIT AND MARSHMALLOW KEBABS

Black Bananas with Butterscotch Sauce

Banana skins are used as natural cooking wrappers in this dessert. Maple syrup imparts a unique flavour to the decadent sauce.

Serves 4

- ❖ 55 g/2 oz butter
- ❖ 85 g/3 oz soft brown sugar
- ❖ 90 ml/6 Tbsp maple syrup
- ❖ 150 ml/¼ pt double cream
- ❖ 2.5 ml/½ tsp vanilla essence
- ❖ 4 large bananas

Put the butter, sugar and syrup into a pan and heat slowly until the butter has just melted. Stir in the cream and vanilla essence. Keep warm (place on the very edge of the barbecue).

Put the unpeeled bananas on the barbecue and cook over a medium heat for about 15 minutes, turning once or twice, until black all over.

Lift the bananas on to a plate. Make a slit along each one, pulling the skin back gently.

Drizzle with some sauce and serve the rest separately.

Pan-Fried Apples with Apple Brandy

*French apple brandy is made from apples grown in the orchards of Normandy.
Here, it imparts its distinctive flavour to the lightly-spiced apples.*

Serves 4

- ❖ 4 medium eating apples
- ❖ 55 g/2 oz butter
- ❖ 5 ml/1 tsp ground cinnamon, cardamom or mixed spice
- ❖ 30 ml/2 Tbsp soft brown sugar
- ❖ Juice of half a lemon
- ❖ 30 ml/2 Tbsp Calvados or brandy

Halve the apples lengthways and remove their cores. Cut each half into four wedges.

Heat the butter in a large frying pan or wok until melted. Stir in the spice. When the butter is sizzling, stir in the apples and cook over high heat, tossing them once or twice, until golden brown.

Move the pan to a cooler part of the barbecue and stir in the sugar and lemon juice. Heat gently until the sugar has dissolved.

Remove the pan from the heat, pour the Calvados over the apples and serve.

Tip
Serve with whipped cream or thick yoghurt.

Gingered Pears

*These pear halves are good served with a generous scoop of
chocolate ice cream.*

Serves 6

- ❖ Butter, for greasing
- ❖ 3 large ripe pears, peeled, halved and cored
- ❖ 3 pieces crystallized ginger in syrup, drained and finely chopped
- ❖ 45 ml/3 Tbsp syrup from the ginger
- ❖ 45 ml/3 Tbsp ginger wine

Butter six large sheets of thick foil. Lay a pear half on each. Gather the foil around them.

Mix the remaining ingredients together and spoon over the pears. Seal the parcels, pouch style. Cook over a medium heat for 10 to 12 minutes, or until warmed through. Serve immediately.

Toasted Spiced Cake with Warm Berries

*Use any mix of berries you like in this dessert, or just one if you prefer; it
will taste wonderful whatever you choose.*

Serves 6

- 5 ml/1 tsp mixed spice
- 115 g/4 oz butter, melted
- 6 slices of Madeira cake,
  each about 2.5 cm/
  1 in thick
- 675 g/1½ lb mixed fresh
  berries, such as

strawberries, raspberries,
redcurrants,
blackcurrants and
blueberries
- 30 ml/2 Tbsp apple juice
- 30 ml/2 Tbsp caster sugar
- 30 ml/2 Tbsp Crème de
  cassis

Stir the mixed spice into the butter and lightly brush it
over both sides of the cake slices.

Put the berries into a pan with the apple juice and sugar.
Heat gently until the sugar dissolves and the juices begin
to run from the fruit. Move the pan to a cool area of the
barbecue and stir in the liqueur.

Cook the cake over a medium heat for about 1 minute on
each side, or until lightly toasted. The cake burns easily, so
watch it closely.

Serve the toasted cake with the warm berries spooned
over the top.

Hot Fruit Kebabs with Maple Cream

*If you haven't served kebabs as the main course, now is your chance. You cannot
lose with this combination of apple, apricot, banana and fig – it's so wonderful.*

Serves 6

- ❖ 300 ml/½ pt double cream
- ❖ 15 ml/1 Tbsp maple syrup
- ❖ 1 red-skinned apple, halved, cored and cut into six wedges
- ❖ 2 bananas, peeled and thickly sliced
- ❖ 12 fresh lychees, peeled and stones removed
- ❖ 3 fresh plump figs, quartered lengthways
- ❖ 30 ml/2 Tbsp clear honey
- ❖ 25 g/1oz butter, melted

Put the cream and maple syrup into a bowl and whip
lightly to form soft peaks. Cover and chill.

Thread the fruit on to six skewers. Stir the honey into the
butter and brush all over the kebabs.

Cook the kebabs over a medium-high heat for about
10 minutes, turning frequently and brushing with any
remaining honey mixture, until the fruit is slightly
scorched and heated through. Serve immediately with
the maple cream.

Cinnamon Oranges with Orange Liqueur

Oranges provide a refreshing accent at the end of a meal, especially after a barbecue which might have been quite a drawn-out affair. These sliced oranges are well worth the wait.

Serves 6

- ⬧ **6 oranges**
- ⬧ **45 ml/3 Tbsp soft brown sugar**
- ⬧ **2 cinnamon sticks**
- ⬧ **30 ml/2 Tbsp orange liqueur, such as Grand Marnier or Cointreau**

Cut the peel from the oranges, removing all the white pith. Slice each orange horizontally into rings. Lay each sliced orange on a large square of thick foil. Scatter each with 7.5 millilitres/½ tablespoon sugar. Break each cinnamon stick into three and add a piece to each parcel. Sprinkle with the liqueur.

Close the parcels, securing the seams well, then cook over a medium heat for about 10 minutes until warmed through. Serve immediately.

MENU IDEAS

*When you are planning a special occasion, it's handy to plan a menu where each course
complements the others. Perhaps you enjoy a barbecue with a special theme (why not encourage your
guests to join in by dressing up and bringing along an appropriate wine?). Sometimes, it's a good idea
to keep just one course for the barbecue (consider cooking several desserts on the barbecue after a
buffet lunch or supper). Here are some menu choices to make your mouth water.*

Vegetarian Menu for Six

✍

Garlic Bread

✍

Grilled Vegetable Platter

✍

Couscous with Apricots and Pistachios

✍

Glazed Pineapple with Coconut
Rum Cream

Vegetarian Menu for Eight

✍

Roasted Wrapped Baby Vegetables

✍

Kidney Bean Burgers with
Pepper and tomato
(serve with plenty of green salad)

✍

Two-Tomato Salsa

✍

Black Bananas with Butterscotch Sauce

Trout for Four

Corn on the Cob with Shallot
and Herb Butter

Trout Wrapped in Smoked Bacon

New Potato Salad with Creamy Dill
Dressing

A salad of sliced tomatoes with an oil-
and-vinegar dressing

Hot Fruit Kebabs with Maple Cream

Fish Menu
for Six

Tuna and Scallop Brochettes

Grilled Salmon with Warm Tomato Salad

Classic Coleslaw

Toasted Spiced Cake
with Warm Berries

Mediterranean Menu for Six

❧

Warm Tomato and Herb Bruschetta

❧

Souvlaki

❧

Mango and Red Onion Salsa

❧

Rice Salad with Feta Cheese Dressing

❧

Cinnamon Oranges with Orange Liqueur

Another Mediterranean Menu for Six

❧

Potato and Onion Grills with Olives

❧

Lamb with Mustard and Thyme Crust

❧

Tabbouleh with Mango

❧

A salad of baby tomatoes and thinly sliced onions

❧

Nectarines with Orange and Almond Butter

Steak for Eight

⁓

Roasted Sweet Potatoes with Herb and Cinnamon Butter

⁓

Fillet Steaks with a Juniper Crust

⁓

Calypso Rice

⁓

A salad of mixed green leaves

⁓

Lemon Baked Bananas with Citrus Mascarpone

Chicken for Eight

⁓

Vegetable and Sourdough Kebabs

⁓

Maple-glazed Chicken

⁓

Calypso Rice

⁓

Warm Tropical Fruit Salad

An Oriental Flavour for Six

⁓

Indonesian Pork Brochettes

⁓

Chinese Vegetable Stir Fry

⁓

Teriyaki Steaks

⁓

Gingered Pears

INDEX

Barbecue Suppliers

Look for barbecues, fuel and accessories in hardware shops, DIY stores, garden centres, supermarkets, department stores and camping shops. Petrol stations often stock disposable barbecues and fuel. The best choice is usually available during late spring and the summer.

Contact the manufacturers at:

Campingaz. Freephone stockist number 0800 317466

Char-Broil International, 93 Tettenhall Road, Wolverhampton WV3 9PE. Tel: 01902 310136

Landmann Ltd, PO Box 28, Kidderminster, Worcestershire DY12 2EZ. Tel: 01299 250909

Odell, Aber Park Industrial Estate, Aber Road, Flint, Flintshire CH6 5EX. Tel: 01352 762061

Outdoor Chef Ltd, Clockhouse Lane, Belfont, Feltham, Middlesex TW14 8QA. Tel: 01784 421006

Weber Barbecues, c/o Erin-GARDENA, Astonia House, High Street, Baldock, Hertfordshire SG7 6PP. Tel: 01462 895511

Other good suppliers:

British Gas Energy Centres. Freephone 0800 850900

Lakeland Limited, Alexandra Buildings, Windermere, Cumbria LA23 1BQ. Tel: 015394 88100

The Barbeque Shop, 46A Portsmouth Road, Cobham, Surrey. Tel: 01932 866044

Credits

*The Publishers wish to thank the following
for their contributions to the making
of this book:*

Black Knight Barbecues
*Farleigh Hill
Tovil, Maidstone
Kent ME15 6RG
For kindly lending a selection of
barbecues and equipment for
photography in the
introductory section.*

Camden Garden Centre
*2 Barker Drive
St. Pancras Way
London NW1
For the loan of a cast iron barrel
barbecue and charcoal, used to
prepare some of the recipes
and featured in several of the
recipe shots.*

Life File
*For supplying the background
images used on pages 18-19,
28-29, 44-45, 58-59, 76-77,
94-95 and 110-111*

*And to **Diana Steedman** and
Gwydwr Leitch
for lending their trusty barbecue
tools and accessories.*